The Will to Rule by Whose Authority?

The Will to Rule by Whose Authority?

ANDREI YAKIMOV

THE WILL TO RULE BY WHOSE AUTHORITY?

iUniverse books may be ordered through booksellers or by contacting:

iUniverse
1663 Liberty Drive
Bloomington, IN 47403
www.iuniverse.com
1-800-Authors (1-800-288-4677)

ISBN: 978-1-5320-4917-0 (sc)
ISBN: 978-1-5320-4918-7 (e)

Library of Congress Control Number: 2018905893

Print information available on the last page.

iUniverse rev. date: 05/11/2018

Contents

PART I

The Essence of Civilization

At, the dawn of time, a caveman stood at the entrance of the cave, looking out, saw the light, felt the warmth of the sun; saw the awesomeness of the land—its beauty and its vastness; was moved to tears, he felt part of it, and said: this, is my land, this is where I belong; I'll not perish, I'll live on it forever! Is this, caveman's vision, commitment and daring, that reflects his will to survive, and with a conscience to carry out this commitment—his state of civilization?

Much later on, we, see a man standing by the river Tigris, looking at the fields, that he was plowing and said—it is good—I'll stay here forever—this is my land!

After, a long time passes, we see a man on the street of Hella's Athens—as he stood, looking about, he said, here, I am, a human being and went ahead and proved it; with determination, reason, imagination, intuition, will and inner energy!

Now, we are, in New York City, we see a man standing on 5th Avenue, looking at the window display, and said: I want this now, and much more later; and there was more—he build bigger and faster machines, bigger Incs., to help him produce more—consume even more, on credit, and as he contemplates what to buy, he becomes aware that there is many more like him—today—than yesterday—He wonders about tomorrow!

These, four men, that stood on this Earth, at different times and different places—representing vastly different epochs of human history—all four, trying to survive and live, searching meaning and purpose in their particular existence.

Who is the civilized one? who shall say? and on what basis?

The first, one, saves the human race from extinction!

The second, one, gave man permanency, security—security from starvation, belonging and being one with nature.

The third, one, gave us reason and will to be free; to create beauty; to think, to inquire, contemplate, imagine not only our own reality of being, but the universal reality as well.

The fourth, one—the Modern Man—what does he do? He invents, innovates, things—makes them bigger, faster, and makes them on mass, for mass consumption—use and throw-away. He builds mega-cities, where, we now, live in the clouds—watching T.V. and 'computing' on our pc's.

These, four men, it seems, have very little in common, they represent different epochs of human history; where the means of survival are different; but, their commonality lies in their nature of being the same specie—The Human Kind—all dealing, struggling with the Art of how to survive—live a life with integrity and purpose. The methods and the means are very different but the purpose is one!

The beginning of our civilization, is very difficult to ascertain, precisely; however, it is connected with the time, when man began to be aware of being different from the other, living species, and began to think and act, as such—developing, with time, his own distinct and unique character. He, realizes, that he possesses different categories of being: the senses state of being; the mental state of being and the psycho-spirit state of being. With this sense of awareness of his uniqueness, he, in time, establishes his complete state of differentiation; and with this "new" identity, he acquires 'new'—innate need to excel, as a human being. He begins by concentrating on the development of his Being—developing, acquiring an understanding of his environment and beyond—learning to apply this 'new' knowledge/wisdom for the betterment of his own situation and that of his clan/tribe, etc.

It is somewhere, during the time of his awakening and subsequent actions as differentiated being that his civilizing process begins—that is, when, the call of the wild, he could ignore. From this, we should not infer that, this process of civilizing is either, continuous, nor deterministic. It is a random thing—it begins, grows and falls—in different places/times in Man's history. We, cannot infer, just because we, are the last ones, that our, current civilization is better, than all the preceding ones. There, is no historical progressivity—for the differences in civilizations—chronologically speaking—is a matter of degree rather than of kind—since our potentialities and capacities, as humans, is one. After all, it was the Barbarians, that put an End to the Glory, that was Rome!

The Dynamics of a Civilization

The explanation of how civilizations develop is based on the principle of duality of forces, which are contraries to each other, and yet, are inseparable, neither, can, completely destroy the other. One force, is passive, the other is the active—the active, acts upon the passive; and as a result of this clash, a change in the existing reality, will occur, moving towards the creation of a 'new' reality—that is presumably, on a higher level of Being/Existence—hence, we have a progression—progressivity in the state of Being. These, 'new' realities, appear in different varieties: According, to Empedocles—a Hellene philosopher—435 BC, believed that the Universal changes are the results of such clashes—harmony vs. discord—"combine the indestructible material particles into varying forms—constituting the rhythm of the universe". The Chinese Cinic World—independently, came-up with a similar proposition/theory—the ying-yang process—the ying—the static/passive force; the yang—the dynamic/active force. Their interactions, however, is not that of the opposites, rather, each ascends into the other, reaches the point of no-further, and then the process reverses course, until, the opposite point of no-further is reached. Thereafter, the flows become a series of permanent repetition. Example, light vs. dark—the shadows/darkness, gives way to light, and light gives way to darkness. These, type of opposites that are ebb and flow of/to each other represent actual realities and their dynamics does not create new realities; it's 'constant' continuity, is useful as predictive tool—example, the seasons, and the like, situations, that are determined, by natural sources and forces—e.g. The sun, Earth's rotation, etc., that are greater, planetary force—given realities, and as, such, they in themselves have no-self, no voluntary actions or reactions, to each other. Their, pattern of behavior is already determined—establishing their precise—repetitive pattern/rhythm of behavior. Since, these, 'dualistic' forces are a function of other—greater forces and have no deterministic action, of their own; it is therefore, pointless to categorize them as dualistic contraries.

If, on the other hand, we take the universe—representing the origin and the prime source and energy, then, the contraries principle will apply; since, the interaction/clash between the opposites; static vs. dynamic; integration vs. differentiation; definite vs. indefinite; finite vs. infinite, etc., (as H. Spencer, points out) will result, in an identifiable and predictable pattern/rhythm of creation and destruction of the new and the old worlds/planes!

There, is however, another school of thought, that attempts, to explain, Reality, by the process of Dialectics; whereby, the clash of the opposites will create a motion, and that motion, in-turn, will cause a change in the now reality—whatever, that change is, it represents, our new, reality. Empedocles, began this line of inquiry, but he, did not develop a convincing method to support his argument—as I stated, before, He said, that, two opposing forces combine indestructible material particles into varying forms—i.e., creation of new reality. Friedrich Hegel (1770-1831), German philosopher, developed, what we know today, as "The Hegelian Dialectic", which had an enormous world influence, especially to the Socialists. Marx, using Hegel's Dialectical reasoning, as a basis, developed his own Dialectical Materialism theory. Hegel, maintains. that, there is a universal perpetual self-creating process, driven by the envelopment of the Absolute. The perpetual rhythm of creation, on ever rising levels, indicates a qualitative progressivity, but this improvement, is at the expense of the previous 'lower' level of existence. If this, is the Universal Dynamics—where, the new—to exist, the old must die. This, principle, precludes the possibility of a universal differentiation, and universal expansion; the two, fundamental characteristics of Universal Reality—for there is no Universal Beauty, without their existence!

The logical process of his dialectics—consisting of the opposites: there is one concept—the thesis—there is also, the antithesis, whereby, they inevitably will interact and create the synthesis—the new reality, the new thesis,—which is on a higher level of being/existence; and has, its own opposite—the new, antithesis, where, they in turn will collide and create, new opposites—this renewal process of creation and destruction, repeats itself, indefinitely, continuously, creating new reality(ies), but at the expense of the existing reality—the thesis, which is "no longer a being", that is, "the idea of being evokes the idea of not being"—the old dies, so that the new may exist. It is the current/now thesis, that is the Absolute and is the active partner in the process—it envelopes the passive—the antithesis— partner into submission, resulting in a new thesis—reality. It is very much like, when the soul envelopes/yokes, the body, creating the spirit-man, moving "from aesthetic contemplation to that of a moral responsibility"— an act of Faith—"the realization of man's spiritual progress". Hegel, sees, this spiritual development in a historical perspective, and as a "necessary manifestation due to the clashes of cultures", whereas, Kierkegaard, sees it as a "free will" in action, "where every man must decide for himself whether he will do the ascendency"—it is by "direct intuition", that one can "understand his own self". That is, only by "immediate experience"— passing through "dark night of the soul"—in anguish, can we know, what it means to be or not to be"—knowing your own conscious existence. Not, as Hegel, wants us to believe, that it is a continuous clash of the opposites going through a mechanized process of dialectics.

These, two approaches, attempt, to explain the nature of human experience: one, sees, man as a free, thinking and acting being—charting the course of his life, according to his desires, beliefs, and means, and as a result of these efforts, he will discover, know, and understand his own being—and thereby develop his capacities and potentialities, realizing his own self, residing in a common environment, pursuing a common purpose—the creation of a more perfect civilization—advancing the human condition!

The other, approach, explains human development, in deterministic patterns of behavior, between opposing forces, clashing in a predetermined phases, resulting in and creating new realities. The Individual, here, is lost, he is simply an Actor, in a play—he is not real—he is simply reacting to an already, predetermined (scripted) reality. A reality, that is not of his own making. Where, is his human interaction and interrelation with other human beings, as human beings? It, does not exist, because, he is, not a free man; in fact, he is chained to the Dialectic Method, that is the True Reality!

Karl Marx—the most extreme,—social theorist (1818), adopted Hegel's Dialectic Method, but, departed from his cultural clashes, and established, his own theory of Dialectical Materialism, that explains, the nature, of social change. It, argues, "that matter is the true reality, and everything else, is derived from matter—and is thereby, explained in terms of matter". Life, he claims, is a "series of contradictions—a negation of negation, present in both things and processes". Marx's main/central idea is that, motion, due to the clash of the opposites—thesis vs. antithesis—causes motion, and that in turn, causes change; the resultant—the synthesis—is the new reality (but, at the cost of the current thesis/reality).

This, Universal and Social Dynamics of a continuous transformation of reality, fails, at least, in three respects: First, it fails to explain the beginning of the first thesis. Second, how, did the antithesis become, a reality; and how, did the process—the clash of the two began—there, must have been a, First Cause, to begin the unceasing process of transformation—the Universal Dynamics! Neither, Hegel nor Marx, provide us with, reasonable explanation. The, how, and on what basis, do we justify, the transference of a scientific determinism of a physical reality, to apply/transfer to a social setting, constituted of human beings. If, anything, that defines man, it is, that his behavior is uncertain and therefore, unpredictable. Dostoevsky, underlines, the truth of this position, by stating, that the most difficult task man, is faced with is to make choices, by creating options, and choosing the Best; but, the best, is it the right choice?—the selection process, carries its own collateral consequence(s)—this is man's irresolvable dilemma! Dialectic reasoning, promises, to free man from, these dreaded decisions—correct, man's human weakness by applying the Dialectic Method. Marx, in fact, is exploiting this human weakness, in order, to gain the political loyalty and support from the working class—the proletariat; setting class against class—the proletariat, pure, hard-working people, exploited by the vicious-evil-greedy capitalists—whose, dialectic time, as the thesis, has run its course; it is time for a new—socialists' thesis, followed—in time—by the ultimate Social thesis—the Communism. A state of existence, where, each citizen, would have reached a level of consciousness—in ethical sense—that he will take only, what he needs, and work, according to his ability. It is then, and only then, that, the "Laws of Social Activity, realized by the proletariat class, will triumph over the, hereto, dominant Laws of Nature"—Marx's Proletariat triumphs over, his Dialectics—an irony, indeed!

It is, indeed, a mystery of the irony, to claim that the fallible triumphs over the inflatable, where, the Natural Law determines progressivity; whereby, just because of the efforts of the proletariat (the least pretentious) class, is capable of reaching a perfect social state; that, can overrule his Scientific Theory of the Dialectic Materialism. A theory, that sees no end to its dynamic process—a process of 'continuous' progressivity, operating in an infinite 'span' of time, otherwise, it becomes invalid by its own logic of negation—perfection is not a state of being, it is a state of always becoming better!

The collapse, of the Soviet Union and China's orientation towards 'guided' capitalism, is a factual proof that Marx's Dialectic Materialism and its corollary—idea of communism, is the greatest historical fiction, ever, written by a man. Arnold Toynbee—English Historian—himself holds, a similar duality point of view, but calls it the "Challenge and Response, sequence of events, that cannot be predicted with certainty". However, he adds a Divine element into the essence of civilization, he states: I do not believe that civilizations have to die...civilizations is not an organism. It is a product of wills". Moreover, "it has a purpose, a duly perceived but divinely ordained purpose". Dr. Toynbee, concludes, that—"History is a vision of God's creation on the move." This creation—drama, that takes place in the Universe, is the result of the interaction between the static and the dynamic forces; it is continuous clashes that establish identifiable pattern of continuous behavior—the rhythm of creation and destruction. Dr. Toynbee believes, that, similar rhythmic patterns, exist and prevail, in our quest to become civilized, human beings. That is civilization and its progressivity, like, the universal progressivity, is a function of the process, of the inherent conflict, that exists, between the contraries—the clash between "static condition and the dynamic activities", is and constitutes, the fundamental condition, that the development of a civilization(s) rests upon. This, sense of dualities at work, is best illustrated and represented by the sinic-"ying-yang" symbol, as the most apt, according to Dr. Toynbee, he states: "because, they convey the measure of the rhythm direct and not through some metaphor derived from psychology or mechanics or mathematics".

Dr. Toynbee, process of civilizing—the "challenge-response" relationship, sounds more applicable to human interactions, is misleading, since, changing a name, does not change the nature of the process itself, especially if we, take into account that the creation and the development of a civilization is "divinely ordained and its purpose is duly perceived." This, even though represents a theological determinism, shows, that his challenge-response process is much more deterministic than he cares to admit.

Besides, his assertion above, that, "History is a vision of God's creation on the move." The sequence of events due to the challenge-response mechanism, it is important to point out that the acting forces are human beings—it is a clash of human-dynamic force acting upon another human-static force—leading to an outcome of winners and losers—the victorious, are the creators of civilizations, and the losers are swept into historical oblivion. This, view of the civilizing process makes it as a function of the existence of a crisis environment—e.g. class struggles. Such, proposition, is grossly inaccurate, since the civilizing process is based on human creativeness—a function of Man's systematic application of his most inner forces and his will power to excel!

> Beauty, in thought, idea and image, cannot be destroyed;
> You, can kill the Artists but, you cannot kill his Art!

Civilizations, I believe, are the consequences and a product of human effort; they, are not ordained nor controlled by the supernatural—nor do they have divine purpose—divine purpose does not change nor fall, civilizations do change and fail. God, really, does not enter nor interferes, with our human intercourses and interactions—that is why, he gave us free will—to act but with consequences.

Civilization, entails a collective human effort, in creating a framework of social structures, whereby, people will live by the Rule of Law, in freedom of thought and action, reflecting the reality now, and the aspirations that, it strives to achieve tomorrow—that is, it defines, man in a social setting in two ways—you, as being and tomorrow, as becoming. The subject, is man, the object, is his becoming; the two, are separate by time, but are inseparable by essence, since, man as a being cannot be defined, as a moment in time; but is defined as a connected series of moments in its totality. The human life is predetermined and it has an end—that is, its nature. The life of a civilization is uncertain, it is not preordained, and therefore, it has no nature of its own. It is a product of man's taught, effort and will—it is what man makes it to be, that is, its Essence. It serves man's purpose, it iŝ man's means towards his purpose. It is that—that,— is moving through time, the relationship between the subject and the object, creating outcomes—good or evil—that define man, as human phenomena of being!

Civilization can be viewed, as having the identical patterns, in its evolving—'creative' process of becoming, and eventually of being—if the objectives are realized—however, it has no definitive end, as man has. The difficulty with history is that we see and study Man—his civilization—in antecedant order, rather, than in its natural order of development; and, since, we know—already—its final outcome, we miss a great deal of its evolving journey of becoming. It is in the evolving process of becoming that the civilizations' creations/destructive urges reside. The evolving process of creativity is the conflict between what is—customs, tradition, habits, and what is missing/desired. The urges to redress the missing/wrongs of society, challenges the status-quo, creating a conflict—struggle ensure— the series of such conflicts, will determine the state of civilization—the transition between yesterday—the past and the tomorrow—the future, is the responsibility, of today—now; yesterday, is history, tomorrow, is uncertain, today, is real, but the time is so short!

Dr. Toynbee, maintains that, human "history is not a sum total of series of forces at work, but a series of human relationships, which create a change, and in this change, it is hoped, will be a creative one, that will shake part of mankind out of the 'integration of custom' into the differentiation of civilization".

All things change, but not at the same constant rate, and therefore, in time, imbalances will occur, in our Goals, in our Means and in our Motives, that will inevitably, alter the fundamental foundation, on which the hopes and the expectations of the new generation(s) rest. New generations are born, grow and mature, bringing with them: new ideas; new thinking; new desires; new needs, new hopes; new inventions and new ambitions, etc. They will formulate their own visions of their tomorrow, with their own commitment, of—energy, will, and conscience to carry-out this commitment.

All, civilizations are different and unique, in their own right; but, they All share three things that are in common to All: their beginnings, start with an 'Idea—a purpose'; their beginning and becoming processes are similar, if not, identical, and they, all face their inevitable End only, the duration of time varies. Civilizations, unlike the confluence of tributaries of small rivers, joining together, to form the great river; they, individually— each, has, created something unique, that succeeding civilizations, have benefitted—but, only as means and not as, foundations, that constitute an a priori condition(s) for the development of the new civilization(s). Historical, continuity of All civilizations, is an illusion, based on the idea of class conflict—propagated by the Communists.

Nonetheless, we, gain, enormously, by their:—ideas, discoveries, experiences,—that, we incorporate in our lives. From, the Chinese, we, learned the concept of Money—that moves our commercial world; their discovery of the gun-powder that the west turned into military weapon.

From, the Hebrews, Moses, gave us the 10 Commandments—that is the basis for our sense of Morality, and the idea, that, there is, only, one God. From, the Arabs, we learned the importance of the zero; the idea of immortality—that is the foundation of all Faiths; their, use of hieroglyphic writing, led to the development of our western alphabets—that, enables us, to develop our unique and distinct language—that defines and expresses our national history and future aspirations. Hellenes, taught us, the idea of Beauty, Individualism, Democracy, the sense of Universal Ideas, Laws, that are immutable, etc. Romans, taught us that: one man, cannot rule the world, based on the idea that might is right, and that the unity of any State/Empire cannot be maintained, if that State/Empire is divided into two classes—Patricians and the Plebeians. The Early Christians, taught us that Faith in God, is the greatest Force of All!

The above, few, but important examples of what we have inherited from past civilizations—they, constitute the common threads that binds us, all, as human beings—they are means/lessons that we adopted or failed to adopt, to help us develop a better world. In our journey of discovering the Truth, we have gone through different Ages and phases of human interactions to achieve that goal. The struggle has been between those that Rule and the masses that they rule—oppression against freedom!

The Purpose

The real purpose of a civilized society, is the realization of the following objectives, for its people:

<u>One</u>: Fulfillment—the required condition for, the uplifting of the human spirit, enabling the Individual to live a meaningful life, and in-time discovers the life's purpose.

<u>Two</u>: Enlightenment—the necessary condition for the realization of man's Essence.

<u>Three</u>: Refinement—the required condition for the enablement of man's soul.

<u>Four</u>: Faith—man's eternal hope—for eternity—that sustains his purpose in life!

<u>Five</u>: The Nature of Man—His:
   A. Life—the state of Being
   B. Liberty—the condition of Being
   C. Essence—the purpose of Being

These, are, then the necessary factors for man to acquire, in order to fully develop and achieve complete understanding of one's own condition as a civilized human being.

Motives

Generally, speaking, it is accepted, that Man is motivated by two, distinct and separate motives: The first, is our sense of Morality. It is Faith based, our belief in the Divine Authority. Our nature, is divinely inspired and determined, and, in that sense, we have a speck of the divine in us—call it, will or conscience or both. Whatever, it is, it is, the force that, enables us to know and understand, what is 'good' and what is 'evil'. They are the opposites of each other, and are not the absence to each other. As opposites, they are in conflict—war—with each other; and, since both—are part of our being, they, in turn, determine our behavior. If our acts and deeds are of the good—kind—we are said to be good, and, if our acts and deeds are of the evil-kind, we are said to be evil. Goodness, reflects God's Goodness and Kindness, which, if we emulate, we'll be blessed with His Grace and go to Heaven. Evilness, on the other hand, reflects the Devil's evilness and depravities; which, if we act accordingly, we'll end up in Hell forever. Whether, we go to Heaven or go to Hell depends—solely—on the Individual, he, decides, how to act and behave; these decisions are not easy, they involve our innermost emotional, agonizing, conflicting and contradictory feelings, that make it impossible to know, with certainty, what is Good and what is Evil. This struggle reflects and constitutes the Essence of our Morality—the strongest and the most enduring motive of human behavior—that is of global proportions and historical endurance.

Its strength and endurance lies in the fact, that, it straddles and connects the finite with the infinite and our material world with the world of tomorrow—the spirit world!

The second, motivating force is Man's Ethics, arising from his inner instincts and drives—the need to survive—instinct, that causes man to be Egocentric. And, on-the-other hand, his propensity to procreate—the force, that causes man to be Altruistic—a life/existence, with others, in a common social setting, under collective social rules—your actions, must be in consideration of others. It is in this collective environment, where, the Individual is cautiously placed in conflict with, his own inner feelings and drives; and in order to resolve this conflict between his need to survive Egocentrism, and his desire to exist with other—Altruism—he is forced to seek a balance between the two, but that balance is possible only, if the individual—willingly or by compulsion—is ready to compromise, but comprise is indeed, difficult. Egocentrism, is a very powerful motive for/of behavior, since, it is based on and reflects a very basic and simple reality—the truth is, that, if I do not look after myself—my interests—nobody else, will—the I, to survive and live well, the I, must, look after itself. This fact, splits, the I from the collective whole—it is a case of I vs. Them! And, in order to survive, in this world, I must, acquire power, influence and prestige, by amassing wealth—by being Greedy. But, greed, is the very antithesis to Altruism—the fundamental condition for the creation and the existence of any Society. Therefore, any society to survive and flourish must apply coercive methods to reduce and possibly, eradicate the greed-based motives, that split the harmony of the collective whole—but the method(s) used, 'may' punish and penalize, the creative excellence of the motivated few! The 'collective will', has yet, to find a convincing—simple argument, to serve, as a motivating force—for all of its members—to induce each member, to apply himself, as if, he is working for his own interest; unfortunately—as of now, such incentive does not exist.

Attempts, have been made to appeal to our sense and belief in humanity—we are All Brothers—hence, we are All our Brothers' keepers—a sense of generosity and obligation—this becomes awkward to both, the giver and the receiver—the giver, feels good and superior and the receiver feels, inferior and loss of dignity. The appeal based on morality—be kind to our fellow man, is a faith-related concept, and is based on selfish motives, to enhance, your chances of getting into Heaven. These are motives that evoke pity rather than purposeful and noble action(s).

Altruism, as a civilizing motive/force leads one, to conclude, that, the welfare of the Individual is a function of the Will of All, and the moving force—the Social Dynamics—is Adoption. The opposite applies to Egocentrism, as a motive/force to civilize, leads, one to conclude that the survival of All, is a function of the Creative Excellence of the Few; and the Driving Forces, here are the quest for gain and competition. Creation and the development of civilizations, is possible, but only, when the positive/creative forces/drives of morality and Ethics, overwhelm and prevail over their negative/destructive counterparts: that is, when goodness penetrates and mellows the inner drives of the Individual, thereby directing his creative impulses towards constructive acts and deeds. To supplement the civilizing drive, the process must be complemented by an equal creative drive and direction by the state, to offset the evils' detrimental penetration into the Ethics of Social Conduct. Society, therefore, must find and implement countervailing measures to dampen—eradicate, if possible—such destructive influences, acting on the social fabric. These, corrective measures, however, must not be done at the expense and the detriment of the positive/creative motives and influence.

The balance, between Egocentrism and Altruism—i.e., fairness and motivation, must exist, but, it ought never be tilted against the Individual, for, it is his will and conscience that constitutes civilization's Drive and Energy.

Sources

In order to achieve the stated objectives, that civilization demands, motives, alone are not enough. We, need Resources-Natural, Human, Social and Spiritual, that will enable us, to provide the necessary goods and services, for the satisfaction of the stated objectives. The Natural

Resources—Land, Water, Climate, raw materials, gas, oil, machinery, transportation markets—constitute our opportunities, but their shortages, will determine our limitations, as well. Their, efficient application, in the production of needed Food, is of vital importance, since, it will determine the extent to which Society will be able to free its Labor Force to pursue, more creative endeavors, in an Urban Setting—environment, rather than remain on the Land to produce, just enough to feed one-self. The development and the existence of an Urban life is a function of the Rural Efficiency to produce sufficient surpluses, to feed the Urban population and thereby, enable it, to remain Urban.

The efficient use—the allocation and the coordination,—of All of the Resources, will be done by human effort—that itself, will have to be trained, to deal with variety of skills, that will be required, to enable the State, to produce and distribute the finished goods and services, but, also the efficient allocation of its Labor Force, in-a-way, that will ensure, the development of a Civilization that it has envisioned for itself. In the pursuance of this Goal, the society, must, establish the required social framework of institutions, creating the positive environment, to ensure that, the Individual, is free to follow his own, independent, course of action—in determining his life, his faith, his thoughts, hopes and dreams—in a free and open society, that values human life, dignity and respect!

Built-In Constraints

We, can, also, define civilization as the Man's Journey through Time,— living in a collective environment, where, he, as an Individual, is continuously challenged to readjust, his attitude, belief and actions, to an ever-increasing collective whole—as the collective whole gets bigger and bigger, he, in respect to it, gets smaller and smaller, where, his stature and significance, diminishes, accordingly, thereby, creating a society, comprised of weaklings. As a consequence of this, a degradation in the creative pool will occur, reducing society's creative will and energy, which is the essential ingredient, required for a steady development of a civilization. Here, we find ourselves in a paradoxical dilemma—as the collective whole increases, its creative pool of Energy and willpower decreases—the two forces are inversely related—since, their needs to 'exist' are opposite to each other. The collective whole, to function, effectively, requires and rests on Discipline Uniformity and Order; whereas, the Creative Genius, requires and rests on Freedom and Individuality. One, requires stable centripetal motion to hold the whole together; the other, thrives on centrifugal motion to shake-up the status-quo—to move, society—in a more—dynamic state of social action and Individual interactions in order to establish, new—more progressive—Direction. To avoid, sliding into this build-in social dilemma, it is necessary, that a harmonious balance between the two Forces is established and maintained, to ensure, the progressive development of its own civilization.

The other, build-in, civilizing constraint—related to the above, but, is more Kafkasian in nature, deals with the systems' centralization of public and industrial services, and its effects on the Individual—his attitudes, behavior and performance. The process of human interaction, is subjected to overburdening man, with mass-Institutionalization, of human life,—that lends itself to the cause-effect analysis; whereas, human interactions are based on the challenge and response series of actions. These two, realities exist in the same collective environment, dominated by the powers of centralizations, where, even though, they are staffed with human beings—that act as tools for the incorporated entities—they, become more inanimate, impersonal—unfeeling/soulless instruments of the public and the Industrial will. The Individual, in this mass world, becomes, isolated, insecure, anxious and hopeless. All these, causes him to become more and more self-absorbed—Egocentric, satisfying his instinct needs at the expense of all the other requisites for a meaningful human existence.

The next impediment to a steady growth of a civilization, is the Generation Gap—the now, generation, always, rejects the ideals, values, beliefs, and the achievements of the previous Generation; as being outdated, out-of-style, passé, and more or less irrelevant. They, are fascinated by the 'new'—it is accepted as better; and yet, they do not know the long-term consequences of everything new that is a result of science and technology—e.g. The invention of the car, at the time, was seen as a deliverance—freeing man from the horse-moving man, one more level away from the animal world—and it was an example, as, a marvel of man's progress; but, now it is viewed as a dangerous pollutant and a necessity, to earn one's living. The creation of things on mass and the building things on mega scale, is unsustainable, contrary to human nature, and insanely, wasteful—the, new, is infinite, but our resources are finite! Instead, of doing, all we can to curb man's appetite for more—his egocentrism—to prevent the impending disaster, we are, on the contrary, doing everything possible to encourage and keep him to do the wrong things—even finance his mass consumption indefinitely—bury him in Debt.

The disconnect between the past—the known, and the future—the unknown, is an interesting phenomena. The known, can be criticized, praised, but, it cannot be changed—the sacrifice/cost has already been made—it is what it is! The future, on the other hand, is unknown, it can be, what you wish it to be—idealized, hopeful and perhaps, feared. It is a build-in confidence and exuberance of youth, to prove itself, that it is stronger, brighter and better than the older generation—it, will succeed, where, the old failed, it will build a better world for All. This, urge to excel, is based on some sort of an ego-trip—'I am better than you', or, perhaps it reflects an accumulation of suppressed inner feelings and frustrations of failures and insignificance—as exemplified by Father-Son-Mother-Daughter relationships. This conflict takes place now, but the relationship between the combatants is a generational one—it is between the past—tradition and the future—change. That is, what is vs. what is to be; the certain vs. the uncertain. The promise of tomorrow, of course, has its own dramatic appeal—everything is possible; however, the youth, forgets that, the foundation of the uncertain tomorrow is the certain yesterday—tomorrow is impossible without yesterday, hence, yesterday is an a priori condition for the existence of tomorrow, and therefore, it cannot be rejected as irrelevant—few, sons have rejected their Fathers' inheritance!.

The inference, by the New Generation that everything they do and create is better than, what the Old Generation did—that, there exists a direct relationship between what is new and that it is better—i.e. the new qualitatively is superior to the old. That is, that there exists a progressivity in the Human Condition. This, progressivity argument based on Science and Technological advancement, makes 'some' sense, in terms of higher standard of living (for limited few) reflecting material consumption, but does not, in any meaningful way, imply, that we as human beings—in terms of our quest for a meaningful existence and purpose in that existence, are better off today than our forefathers yesterday—just because we live longer and there is many more of us, does not mean that we are better human beings—I would, suggest that the opposite is the case. Whatever, the case may be, the conflict is unnecessary and disrupts the steady—uninterrupted—development of our civilization.

Another, impediment that adversely affects the development of a civilization is based on and reflects our sense of spirituality—that aspect of our inner motives/drives, that propels us to reach out and touch the stars; escape the confines of our Earthy Limits. Our Faiths/Religions, gives us the opportunity\, to do just that—reach the Heavens, but, it extracts a heavy price. It gives you a promise, but there is always a condition—that works on our conscience, that, we are evil, because, we are animalistic—the Flesh-man—that unbearable Egocentristic characterization—which we cannot escape nor accept. Man, is born naked and alone—nature, made him so—he, is himself and for himself, for his own survival. He is against the rest of the world—he can never win, the fact that makes him always, insecure and suspicious of others and their motives. His nakedness, reminds him of his animalness and that fact, makes him ashamed of himself, hence, the need to cover his nakedness; thereby, the realization of a greater differentiation from the rest of the other animals.

Cover, all you will, the body is the same—it does not change. The perception of a naked body, as being shameful, is shared by the Jerusalem-based Faiths, for different reasons. The Christian Church, holds, that man at birth is incomplete and deficient—he, is a Flesh-man, and as such, he sins; he has no spirit, therefore, he possesses no will nor conscience. He is more animalistic, than being a human—he is a savage/barbarian, and as such he is incapable of being civilized!

To become civilizable, he must become a whole—i.e. The Spirit-man. He must go through a process of initiation and purification—through immersion in or sprinkle with water—the Christian rite of Baptism. This rite, in fact, entails the rejection of Evil-The Devil, and the acceptance of the Good—Christ, the Lord and the Savior. The initiated, after, being purified with the Holy Water and blessed with the Holy Spirit (and most likely given a new name) is now the Spirit-man; and with this Baptism, he receives, two gifts from God—Free will and a Conscience. With all this he is now a complete and sufficient man—i.e. he is a completely differentiated human being. The transformation from the Flesh-man to the Spirit-man, entails the Christian belief that, there exists, homeless souls that seek homes of their own. The Holy Spirit blessing—as the key component of the Baptism—achieves exactly that, it unites the homeless soul with now the "new" Man—i.e. The Spirit-man. The two entities are now completely compatible to co-habit exist in one body—as one. This, is achieved, presumably, by process of 'dialectics', whereby, the homeless soul—acting as an antithesis to the Flesh-man—the thesis, by enveloping Him, causing a new creation—the synthesis, which is the 'new' Spirit-man. This process, however, may not be entirely true, since, it goes against the doctrine of God's creation. God, "creates the world. This world is not God; but it is not evil because it is not God. Being God's creation, it is good." (R.Niebuhr).

The two gifts, that, Christians receive with their Baptism is a very significant aspect of Christian Doctrine. The Free will gift, enables the Christian, now, to take control of his own destiny—the self-determination principle. This principle, however, is based, on strict obedience of the Christian Doctrine—its tenets/creed; failure, to comply with this requirement, carries grave consequences—denial to go to Heaven—redemption, possible in extreme circumstance(s). This, gift of free will—self-determination, shifts, the onus and the responsibility to the Individual, for his taught and actions—if he, chooses wrongly, he will pay for it, if he chooses right, he will be rewarded, accordingly—a principle of behavior, based on, reward and/or punishment. The Flesh-man, was not confronted with such a dilemma of choice; he, as incomplete and insufficient, could not be expected to make the right choice, due to his deficiency in his own creation—it is God's fault, that, he could not differentiate between what is good and what is evil and act accordingly.

In fact, the free will gift, give you the right of choice, but this in-itself does not guarantee the right choice. The right choice is based on the second, gift—the possession of a conscience—that will save him from sinning—since now—he is a spirit-man-he is part of the Holy Spirit and as such, he knows the Truth—an a priori condition necessary for making the right choice—he chooses good over evil!

Thus, the Christian Theological Doctrine resolves the problem of Egocentrism. But, does it? It in fact, may have been encouraged by the Free will gift—giving the Individual the right of self-determination—reinforcing the instinct of survival, that is the prime cause of Egotism and splitting the I from the rest of the world; disturbing the universal unity and harmony—the relativity principle. The conscience gift, may not, be sufficient to offset such-strong-tendency; since, it is based on the a priori, basis of knowing the Truth, to make the right choice. However, knowledge of the truth implies and infers knowledge of God and His Will. Sadly, such knowledge on, an Individual basis does not exist! At best, we have an abstract 'notion' of the existence of such a reality. Moreover, it is very doubtful that Man—physical vs. spiritual—has any universal reach, to adversely affect; its harmony and unity—this influence, belongs to God and God, Alone.

There, is no doubt, that a selfish—egotistic man, stands-in-the-way of collective unity and harmony, conditions required for the development of a stable and progressive civilization. To what extent did the emergence of the cross, succeeded in dampening its adverse effect(s) is, of course, debatable; but we, cannot simply, brush aside its failures/excesses—even, today, the greatest demonstration of greed for material wealth, resides in countries of Christian Faith. Also, science—that questions/disclaims God's existence—is prevalent in the same Christian Lands. This, facts, alone, demonstrate, the weakness in our quest to develop our unique civilization; for, if we weaken our Faith, we are, at the same time, weakening our foundation on which our morality stands. And, once, we lose that foundation, we'll find ourselves, being relegated down to our basic instincts of survival—produce, consume and die—a formula for survival but not for civilizing.

The dynamics of a civilization consists of two double contrary forces/tendencies and their final outcomes/resultants: The first, set of contraries is a resultant of our need of/for stability and permanency—the existence of an Unmovable Centre. The opposite to this requirement is the desire for change—the hope for a better world—which requires the existence and the application of new-dynamic force/energy,—to challenge and affect the current order of things. The second, set of contraries emanates from the necessity—the man to restrain and guide the actions of the heartless; while preserving the Individual's independence and motivation to be, a creative and valuable member to the collective whole. These Individual actions, are viewed, in respect to the requirements of the social totality—where, the single Individual can easily be lost, forgotten or both—where, the collective size, will and action(s) are vast, powerful and absolute, overwhelming its own contrary counterpart. Given, these natural disintegrating forces, as a fact of human existence, it becomes imperatively necessary—as a civilizing apriori condition—to unify these forces into a balanced whole, in order to establish the required basis for the realization of a continuously evolving—stable civilization—in which the four categories of means are sufficient, balanced and applied, in an efficient and effective way—where, no one category—singularly, dominates and controls the other categories of means, nor: where, the others, collectively, dominate and control a single category of the means.

The four categories of means/pillars, that constitute and are responsible for the creation and the progressive development of a civilization, Are:

First: The state of Governance—must be so directed, that its actions must promote/encourage, rather than, stifle creative energy, for it is a central pillar, that holds and controls the collective power and energy.

Second: The state of Cultural Activities—such activities must operate in total freedom-encouraged, promoted and protected by the state—for it is the pillar that represents and is the flowering of the human spirit, and is its, creative force and collective pride!

Third: The state of Commercial Enterprise—the country's commercial status and condition, determine its Economic well-being and constitutes its blood vessels, that is responsible for the creation and the distribution of the wealth of the nation, that sustains and promotes, Human, Scientific, Artistic, Intellectual and Technical Advancement.

Fourth: The state of its Religious Beliefs—which determines society's spiritual vibrancy and its potency, to connect Man to the Highest Immovable Centre, and allows him to hope for salvation and Divine Grace!

Civilizations, have Divine relativity, but are not divinely inspired nor, are they divinely ordained; they, are man created and man determined and, driven by the will of man. They represent and reflect Man's aspirations, achievements, as well as, his failures. And, since by nature, man's environment/surroundings, are finite, his civilizations, must also be finite—i.e. they, like man himself are created, grow, decline and eventually will die.

Vibrant and long lasting civilizations require that, they, at their nascent are found on solid and enduring ground—a vision —a quest for the unreachable star. As, the Egyptians did—a quest for man's immortality— around which they created a pantheon of Universal Gods, and made their King—the Pharaoh—a God (the Sun God)—a supreme and absolute ruler. These, Universal Gods, had Earthy functions, involved, practically in all aspects of Man's activities, including his physical body, itself. High priests, that surrounded the Pharaoh, catered to all of his wishes—his ceremonial duties on this Earth; preparations for the Pharaoh's journey into the Heavens, where, he would join and live in eternity with his brother Gods. An entire culture developed around the idea of eternity: from the world of the living—Nile, as the source of Life,—the Pharaohs glorified and remembered by time, with the unsurpassed Temples at Karnak, Luxor—Western Thebes, etc.

The world of the Dead, their Tombs—The Pyramids/the House of Eternity—mystery to us, even at this present day,—their purpose still, yet unclear, possibly/likely, the interim resting place for the embalmed body, waiting for its departed soul, to be reunited in perfect bliss for eternity, if —Osiris—God of the Underworld—Judges that your heart is truthful and your soul is pure. The Egyptians, believed in perfect Universal Order, where, everything is in Balance and Harmony—a state of perfection, fixed and constant, resting on the Unmovable Centre—The God Creator. They saw being/existence as a continuous process of becoming—as part of the cosmic order—from the physical to the spiritual Realms of existence, both, existing in their own Individual Identities—one, finite, the other infinite—where, the finite is infused into the infinite. Man, is at one, and the same time, being in Heaven and on Earth, as well. There is —exists a mystical KA—the "Immortal" Universal Spirit, part of which resides in each one of us (an idea that appeared in the Christian Doctrine, as the Holy Spirit, millenniums later).

According to Lionel Casson (Ancient Egypt), the Egyptians "beliefs are not solely reflections of mythical imaginations but involve articulate intelligence and will" behind their explanation of the cause of the Act of Creation. Ptah, "conceived the idea of the Universe and executed that idea by uttering a command." The designed creation implies that there is a purpose for each creation, whereby, all acting separately—doing their predetermined roles—will in totality, fulfill the Universal Design. The prime mover—the first principle,—is the Divine God, The Chief God—The Creator of All. It is in this Cosmic Order and purpose that the Egyptians sought to fit their own existence; where, they designed a socio-political structure that immolated the universal system of order and purpose. They made their King, the Pharaoh—a God, brother of the Gods, to create the Immovable Centre on Earth, establishing a total—absolute—and unquestionable Authority, in the person of the Pharaoh. It is in this way, that, they established and justified their legitimacy of Governance. The question of legitimate succession, was a more difficult issues in case, if the reigning pharaoh had no son, what then? To resolve, this difficult dilemma, they reached all the way-up to the chief God, and assigned the responsibility to him, to produce the needed 'heir at-law', by requiring him to sleep with the pharaoh's Queen. Thus, ensuring a legitimate succession and by a Divine-'immaculate' conception: Egyptians, held, that the Gods created a Universe, "precisely in the form they wanted. Everything therefore was just as it should be—fixed, eternal and proper".

The issue of legitimacy to Rule and the heir at-law principle are issues that reflect society's class structure and its antagonistic reality between the Ruling/Elite class and the common class—the people—that is, the will of the Divine vs. the will of the People. History, shows, that, the will of the Divine/Dictators prevailed—even, today, most of the world is ruled by ruthless, power hungry Dictators; giving themselves—on the basis, of might is right—the right to rule, without the consent of the people nor a Divine blessing. Democracy—the peoples' right to choose their own Rulers,—is relatively a new Ideology—handed down to us by the Greeks, has established deep roots only in very limited number of countries; where, the will of the people, determines the 'Ruling Elite'. The problem of Democracy, however, is that it is very divisive, cumbersome—slow—Ideology driven, causing confusion and uncertainties in—the long-run, policy matters. It is uncertain as to which path to take to ensure balance and harmony between the well-being of the Individual and the Public interest—follow, the Competitive—private ownership and control of the Economic Means or follow, the Cooperative—public ownership and control of the same means, or perhaps a mix of the two! Probably, its worst defect stems from its foundation—it rests on an unresolvable paradox its principle of equal participation—one person, one vote—a rule that leads to paradox between fairness of representation and responsibility of contribution to the needs of the Collective whole. Contribution is done by the 'creative few', while, the equality is enjoyed by the masses, and yet, it is the masses that decides who is to Rule! Out of this right to equal participation in the political arena, arises a transference argument, that maintains, that, since, we are—All equal in the political domain, we ought to be equal in all other domains, especially in the wealth domain—hence, and therefore, we All must enjoy the same/equal standard of living, regardless of effort/sacrifice made—the birth of Entitlement—the creation of the welfare state. A program, that was meant to help those in need, on a temporary basis, giving them a chance to get back on their feet, turned into an entrapment of the very same people that it was helping to get better, into a life-long (in some cases generational dependency on the Government dole to survive) without 'any' chance of escaping such ill-designed fate.

In their early dynasties, the Egyptians, developed/evolved with an Ethical sense of right and wrong—a system of Justice—a belief that after life you'll be judged, and judged on the basis of your truthfulness—i.e. the purity of heart and pure conscience. Osiris—the God of the Dead, presides over an elaborate trial, to determine your fate after death, whether, you'll go to eternal life of bliss or you shall be devoured by the hybrid monster. The trial is held in the "Hall of Double Justice", where, on one side of the scale of justice, the heart of the deceased is placed and on the other side is Maat-the Goddess of Truth and Justice—herself or her ideogram—the ostrich feather is placed. There are, also 42 Judges present—representing each province, sitting in judgement of the deceased (equivalent of today's trial by Jury). If the scales are in perfect equilibrium, then Osiris, will render a judgment of free passage into the Kingdom of Osiris, to live with the gods and the spirits of the dead, in eternal bliss. Christian Theology adheres to a similar trial; only, it is Christ-the-Lord of the Universe—sits in Judgment. The difference is that if you are found guilty, you are condemned to 'live' in Hell for Eternity; and of course, the innocent go to Heaven, to live in bliss forever, in God's Kingdom!

Another, similarity between Egyptian Mythology and Christian Theology is the belief in and the understanding of the Trinity Doctrine —a situation where three different entities are united into one—Christian Trinity consists of The Father/God, The Son/Christ and The Holy Spirit. LaRouse Encyclopedia, makes at least two references of the idea of Trinity: God, Osiris—the Fourth Divine pharaoh, was killed by his brother, out-of-jealousy, was resurrected by his faithful and beloved wife-Isis and their son-Horus,—constituted the 'divine' Trinity. The other instance of trinity refers to Ptah—the sovereign God of Memphis, Sekhmet—his wife—the beloved of Ptah and his adopted son-Imhotep formed the 'divine' Triad, during the King Zoser's third dynasty (2686-1613). "It was claimed that Imhotep, was born not of human parents but of Ptah himself."

If we, view and examine the above Egyptian Mythical creations and events—in totality—: their obsession with immortality,—life-in-bliss, after death; Divine creation; were mortals are elevated to Divinity; Resurrection of the dead; Divine Justice, to determine purity of the heart and the conscience of man's soul; and perhaps, the most significant issue, of who or what constitutes the Highest Universal Power and the creator of All—the concept of Trinity!

To us, today, the above concepts, ideas, and beliefs, constitute and represent distant—antiquity, are Egyptian body of knowledge that we term as Mythology. But, if we, take the same body of knowledge today, and applied it to our Christian Faith, we identify it, as Theology. Christianity, in fact, deals with the same body of knowledge, as summarized above, with the exception that it chose monotheism—one God vs. Polytheism, that the Egyptians, believed in. The Egyptians, in fact, did believe in one 'chief God'—the creator of 'All'—as well as the sub-Gods, to help Him Rule the Universe; as Christ had His Twelve Apostles!

The Historical 'Transformation' from, Mythology to Theology occurred in 325, when, Constantine I, was forced to convene and Head the First Ecumenical-Universal-Council to establish, some form of uniformity to the young Faith, that was more of a movement; in disarray and disorder; a movement that was led by Jesus, with a purpose to reform the Jewish Faith—on the basis of his teachings. However, with the crucifixion/ resurrection of Christ Jesus; thanks to St. Paul, that movement; turned into a deliberate, determined spiritual journey. St. Paul transported and spread Jesus' word of the Love, Salvation and Grace to the Gentiles. St. Paul, travelled extensively into the Middle East, the Balkans and visited Rome, four times. It is due to his efforts, that, Jesus' word took roots, grew and turned into a Force-of-Faith—pure, innocent, dedicated and fearless force—withstood and eventually conquered the Roman cruelty, oppression and murder, but was leaderless and disoriented. Its transformation from a movement to an Institutionalized Faith—the establishment of a United Universal Church was extremely difficult, given the fact, that, it was in and under a Roman Empire and its Emperor, who believed himself to be the Absolute Lord of the World—the Earthy Pantocrator—whereby, he considered the Christian Affairs, as only one of his Departments of his Governing Structure. Leaderless and unsure of their Fundamental—Core—Beliefs—i.e., lack of coherent Christian Doctrine. It was for this reason that the Great Ecumenical Council was convened (as explained before) to attempt to establish the needed common core beliefs in the form of Doctrinaire Tenets.

The deliberations, in essence, centered on the Crucial question of the true nature of Jesus. Arius—Priest of Alexandria, argued (as stated above) that Jesus was neither eternal nor equal with God—the Father. Athanasius—Patriarch of Alexandria and Doctor of the Church—vigorously, opposed Arius, arguing that Jesus was one with the Father—begotten...being of one essence with the Father. This view prevailed and was issued as a basic Creed for all Christians. Thus, the first, Ecumenical Council of Nicaea in 325, establishes the Christian Trinity Doctrine, made-up of The Father, The Son and The Holy Spirit. Here, we have a 'Universal Council' made-up of 218 Bishops, led by a Patriarch—Doctor of the Church, Headed by a Roman Emperor, deciding who is Divine—a mortal Man determines and proclaims the Divine! On what basis and on what precedent? The basis and the precedent are both, from past human experience—its reality and Mythology was known to the Christian Theologians—they, simply adopted and transformed the old into the New Faith. There, but exists a fine line between myth and faith; the Universal Faiths, that we take as 'infallible truths', are, in fact, based on and are derived from ancient/antiquity myths. Faith and Myth are intertwined, they are both, the creation of our fears and hopes—our imagination, perception and intuition at work! In either case, they serve as the motivating and moving force for the evolvement and the development of our respective civilizations.

The Ancient Greeks—Hellas—and the Romans in essence and method followed—'in-step with'—the Egyptian Model of Civilizing. The Greeks, however, differed from the Egyptians in their purpose—which was Beauty above all. Their quest for and worship of beauty caused the development of an unparalleled Architectural marvels; their love for wisdom—logic and reason—led to the development of Higher Learning Institutes, where, the Masters of Philosophy, led their students on a journey of discovery of the Truth—the concept of Justice, the very nature and essence of man himself; the advancement of the Arts and Literature; unlike the Egyptians.—who saw eternity in the Universe, they saw, Universal Idea, Universal Spirit, Universal Forces that caused and moved the Universe itself—the idea of duality—cause—effect dynamics, order in disorder; kept their Gods' close to themselves—gave them a place of residence on the top of Mt. Olympus—interacted with them on a human as well as divine level. They left, to posterity, the richest legacy in the history of man—in; taught, reason, word, belief and in the greatness of Man. The Age of Renaissance is, in fact, the re-birth of Greek culture, that enabled the west to develop and enjoy an advanced civilization—the fruits that it brings with it! The greatest gift that the Greeks gave to the world—is not the Trojan Horse—but a new idea of how best to Govern ourselves—the idea of Democracy,—Government by the people—the proposition, that holds, that, it is the peoples' inherent right not only to be free but, to have the right to participate in the selection process of those that will govern them! A new, novel and revolutionary idea, reflecting a period of God's chosen—Absolute—Rulers and Society comprised of antagonistic social classes, etc.,—but, they planted the seed and the seed grew—and we are now reaping the harvest—a harvest of freedom, equal rights—a harvest of human dignity.

Democracy, is not an easy, nor is it inspiring form of Government, it is based on trust and majority rule, which are difficult to accept completely—especially for the losers—it seems, it deals with numbers and counting numbers, rather, than the well-being of the people. Democracy, as a political system attempts to satisfy Aristotle's axiom—that moderation is the Golden Rule—neither too much nor too little. That is, as the Democratic process works itself out, in that very action, we are cleansing the system of the impurity(ies) of the extremes and thus, we are left with the best possible results possible—i.e., that, the best possible results are found in the middle of the political spectrum, where the majority of the people are—reside. The question is, are the two concepts—the majority and the medium one and the same thing or are they different; representing entirely different propositions—majority, represents numerical———abstract—concept/results, whereas, the golden mean represents a qualitative standard—hence, the majority rule cannot and does not represent the 'Best' political results. The beliefs that extremes are always detrimental to peoples' well-being, is not well founded, since, it is the extreme policies—once adopted—become most advantageous/popular to the people, e.g. F.D. Roosevelt and R. Reagan's Revolutions, putting aside, the rational for equality of participation and the ability of the average voter, to be able to select the ''Best' political results, we can say with certainty that, Democracy, is people friendly and is the foundation—The Rock on which Free Men, Stand Firm!

Rome—The Glory of Rome. The greatest Empire hat ever existed, was based on the belief that Rome was destined for greatness, and to fulfill that destiny, the use of power—to subjugate others—was justified. This, unshakable, belief in their greatness, gave the Romans, the quest for the unreachable star. This objective motivated the Romans to prove that they are indeed, Great, created an Empire—indeed two Empires—lasting more than two millenniums, overcoming, enormous difficulties and obstacles, arising from external, as well as, internal forces:

One—Rome's social class structure consisted of—in effect—two classes—the patricians—the nobles, the ruling elite, the Aristocrats, land and slave owners. Opposite, to the elite class, is the class of common people, the plebians—of low birth and station. The two classes had nothing in common and shared no common values nor purpose, except, that they all were Romans. They, in fact, were the antithesis to each other, and this made them protagonists to one another. This inner struggle pushed and propelled Rome to grow from a small Kingdom, to a considerable Republic and then to a Great Empire. It is, however, the Republic, that is dearest to the Roman Hearts, because it recognized the people as human beings and the power rested in the Hands of the Senators—The Senate!

Two—As, Rome, was sliding into a state of Imperium; the Republican System of Government was not sufficient enough to accommodate the needs of the new Empire; it required a greater centralized power base—concentrated in one person—realizing a greater reach; a greater projection; and a greater coordination of power and purpose. This required the building of roads, ships, etc., for faster and more secure transportation of military and commercial ventures—as the Mediterranean Sea became encircled by Roman land forces, in fact, making it the Roman Lake.

Empires, require strong and determined hands to lead and rule the expanding Empire. Rome, never could establish a lasting formula to ensure the Empire's succession policy. In case of an Emperor's death, many contenders appeared, each claiming the right to succession; it was settled in the field-of-battle, where, the victor got the crown—at the end, the crown was worth nothing—it was offered for sale!

Three—Rome, with its Aristocratic attitude and the pride in the Pax Romana citizenship developed a superiority vs. inferiority attitude and behavior towards its northern and western neighbors—seeing them as wild Barbarians—uncivilized creatures; which, made it impossible for Rome to devise a sound-practical policy to live in peace with them. It, in fact, chose a policy of subjugation by conquest of superior force. A struggle, that lasted for centers and ended disastrously for Rome. The Barbarians in 410, sacked Rome; King Alaric of the Visigoths—in 419—found a Kingdom in Gaul; in 455. The Vandals sack Rome; and in 476, Odoacer—Germanic chieftain—deposes the last Western Emperor of Rome; and effectively, puts an end to the Empire—(Great Ages of Man—Imperial Rome—chronology). After their conversion to Christianity, the Barbarians created marvelous Christian states, but misguidedly, misapplied their Economic and Military power to attack and destroy their sister Christian Church—the Orthodox Christians—by destroying the Byzantine Empire.

In 313, Constantine, The Great, grants toleration of Christianity, and in 330, forced to abandon Rome, as the capital of the Empire, builds Constantinople, the new capital of the de-facto, the 'new' Roman Empire—The East Roman Empire or the Byzantium. The two Roman Empires are permanently divided in 395 and are never to be united again! With these major changes, the old pax Romana begins to disappear and the new Europa begins to emerge—but emerge in an entirely different Form, Energy and Spirit.

As Constantine was fashioning his new capital and strengthening the Eastern Front, with the hope that, the day will come when, the East will free the west; the west; however, did not wait for that day, it began to formulate its own future—build on the 'unity' of very unlike partners. The foundation was the Old Roman structure/infrastructure and their well known Justice System; complemented and supported by the pure Christian moral ethics and Divine Spirit—applying a well reasoned attitude towards the Barbarians—and by converting them to the new Christian Faith. It, accepted them as equal members of the universal church. Moreover, the church showed a profound understanding of the Barbarian character—their free and independent spirit, can never be fettered, because, if it is, it will die—thus, it chose to follow t he principle of separation of church and state. That is, affairs, dealing/concerning religious and/or spiritual matters, will be the responsibility of the church, headed by the Chief Pontiff—now, the Pope. Whereas, matters dealing with temporal/secular issues, shall be the responsibility of the state—headed by a Sovereign Ruler—The King. However, the church insisted on two conditions,—respecting the above principle: first, Church services must be conducted in Latin; second, all Kings must be anointed/crowned by the pontifex maximus—The Pope. This, unlikely alliance of the three sectors—bringing together the 'old' foundation, the new energy and the new vibrant spirit, lay the basis for the creation of the new Europe.

This arrangement, initially suited everybody: the church, got its independence from the state (unlike the Christian Orthodoxy in the East) to await the second coming of Christ the Lord,—concentrate on saving souls rather than acquiring worldly riches. It had the power of Coronation as well as the power of Holy Baptism; enjoyed a vindication satisfaction over the 'Old' Roman oppressors; and spiritually, it held the key to the Doors of Heaven! The Barbarians, are Christians, because the Spirit-men—an elevation from the 'almost' animal status—independent to pursue the development of their own states. As far, as the Old Rome was concerned, it had to adapt to the new reality—they became very useful in the Administrative Affairs of the state. With time, the old dies, the new takes over—ushering-in new ideas; new views; new desires; new ambitions, greed, takes over, driving a wedge between church and state; the temptation for worldly wealth was irresistible—for it represented power, influence, control, prestige and respect, while, the church represented and offered something intangible, uncertain, a world unknown—a spirit world, required, that we live our earthy lives according to the requirements of that world—Christ-like life—which, as humans, we are incapable of doing—We, fear, the day of Judgement because, we doubt our own purity of heart and soul!

The triple alliance, became an uneasy rivalry between Church and State—each claimed superiority/pre-eminence over the other; rivalry and jealousy set-in amongst states; new states alliances formed and re-formed, the church guided/manipulated most. It, even reconstituted the Old Roman Glory, with its own Christian Cross—The Holy Roman Empire—in the name of Charlemagne—Charles the Great—The Emperor of the West; King of the Franks (768-814); King of the Lombards, conqueror of N.E. Spain; subjugated and Christianized the Saxons (772-804); defeated the Avars and the Wends. In 800, He restored Leo III to the Papal See; in gratitude the Pope—Leo III, crowned Him the Emperor, of the 'new' Roman Empire—The Holy Roman Empire—on Christmas Day in Rome. This coronation—in gratitude and at the same time deliberate—laid the basis for a permanent division and separation between the two Christian Universal Churches. This event, in effect, was direct and deliberate challenge, not only, to the Christian Orthodox Church but, even more so, to the Emperor of the Eastern Roman Empire—Constantine VII—as the Head of State, as the Roman Emperor of the Entire Roman Empire, as well as the Head of the Christian Church. With a single coronation, Pope Leo III and King Charles, revolted against the inherited pre-eminent position held by the East Roman Emperor since Constantine I—both as Emperor and the titular Head of the Christian Church, and claimed the two titles for themselves!

The Eastern Roman Empire, followed the Roman tradition of Governance, continued by Constantine I (330) based on the imitation of how the Universe is Ruled—One Lord of the Universe, one Emperor on Earth—both, secular, as well as, the spiritual matters are/must be under one Emperor. This, formula fitted—quite nicely,—the Christian Doctrine—Christ, The

Pantocrator—The Lord of the Universe—hence, The Emperor—Lord of the World. The timing of the revolt was perfect; the ambitious Irene—the co-Emperor with her son, Constantine VII—proclaims herself, as the sole Emperor/Empress of the East Roman Empire, after she blinds her son. Pope Leo III, proclaims the Byzantine Throne vacant, since Irene is a woman, and the throne must be occupied by a male—a precedent established by the twelve Apostles—all being male. Pope Leo III, with a single coronation, usurps, not only the Byzantine Crown but, also declares that the Pope—i.e., Himself is the Head of All Christendom—He, in fact, assumes primacy, in all Spiritual Affairs, over the East Roman Empire. This masterful plot, failed because, in Constantinople, the Palace revolted against Irene, and proclaimed Nicephorous, Emperor. The west, was relentless in their drive to subsume the Byzantine Empire and its Orthodox Church, under their control. Another, contentious issue arose, when St. Ignatius—Patriarch— of Constantinople, lost his position; a Greek Theologian was ordained to take his place (858); the Pope Nicholas I, however, refused to recognize him as the legitimate Patriarch of Constantinople, because of his contrary position to the Roman See, on the issue of the Iconoclasm. Photinus, responded by calling the Synod to question and evaluate, some Latin beliefs/customs—in particular—Popes' right to pass judgement on the election of Byzantine Patriarchs. This schism marks the beginning of the End, the split between the two Christian Universal Churches. And, in 1054, the Byzantine Church breaks with the Roman See.

An important—ongoing disagreement, concerning a doctrinarian issue— dealing with the 'proper' relationship between the Son and the Holy Spirit in the concept of the Holy Trinity. The Nicaean Ecumenical Council, declared that—there is a Father/God, the Son and the Holy Spirit—the Son and Spirit enemate from the Father, of course; but the Council, specifically, did not proclaim the exact relationship between the Son and the Spirit,—the Orthodox Church, worked on the inferred premise that the two entities are both Holy, Unique in their own creation and separate—they are co-equal inhabitants of the Holy Trinity. The Catholic See, took a different position, elevating the Son much more closer to the Father—a Divinity, who has been with the Father at the beginning of All creation; must have been and has taken part in the creation of the Holy

Spirit—hence, the Holy Spirit enemates from both the Father and the Son—that is, the Father and the Son are Divine but the spirit is 'only' Holy! John the Baptist, however, tells us that, when Jesus, came down on Earth to save mankind, He waited for the Holy Spirit to arrive and 'empower' Him to perform Baptism, this indicates—clearly—that Jesus did not outrank the Holy Spirit. We, should not forget, the role of the Holy Spirit in the Immaculate Conception of Jesus, Himself! The difficulty here,—as I have argued before—is the concept —the idea, of Trinity itself; and more specifically what do we mean by the idea of the Holy Spirit—Is it an extension (tool) of God, to do His bidding or is it a separate entity, with its own identity, will and purpose? In Jesus' case, according to John, Jesus tells us that He is on Earth to do God's will, not His own. This defines Jesus as a separate, complete being—the Son of the Father, doing His Father's bidding—a Family 'without' a mother, the Egyptian Trinity did have a mother! At any rate the disagreement was never resolved.

The question of primacy, did not go away, the Roman Catholic Church, in order to justify its rightful claim, as the legitimate Head of All Christendom and Rome as the Universal Centre, presented what it calls—the Petrene Supremacy Doctrine—which in effect contends,—that the Pope, is a direct successor to St. Peter, by virtue of Peter's position, as the Chief Pontiff of the Rome's Church and His Cruel death by the Roman Empire; in 67. He is referred to as the prince and the Leader of the twelve Apostles after the crucifixion of Jesus. He is pictured, as holding the keys of the Gates of Heaven. Jesus, after, his Resurrection charged Peter to "feed my sheep". Here, we, see Peter—the rightful successor to Jesus, and His mission—and this, is exactly what Peter endeavored to do—He, ministered north of Jerusalem, Antioch, etc., following in the footsteps of His Master—healing, ministering. Peter, the loyal and trusted friend—defending and spreading 'His Masters' mission of love and peace and His deeds of conversion to salvation. The emphasis is on Jesus' Reform of a corrupt Jewish religion— to transform it—give it Love, Grace and Salvation—which Peter embraced whole-heartedly and pursued. There, was no intent, to start nor create a 'new' religion—only, a serious transformation of the existing one! For this reason, Peter was against the conversion of the Gentiles—because, it was a "matter of required circumcision, that was part of the covenant between Moses and His God", which the Gentiles never practiced. St. Peter, "changed his mind—late in his life", when he decided to go to Rome. Also, the realization of St. Paul's success in the conversion of the Gentiles to Jesus' Faith. This, and much more was happening. St. Paul, believes Himself to be a 'new' prophet, charged by God to carry-out a mission of transforming Jesus' movement into a Faith—transforming Jesus of the Gospels into Christ of Theology". Durant, explains—"Paul had found a dream of Jewish eschatology, confined in Judean Law; he had freed and broadened it into a faith that could move the world…interwoved the ethics of the Jews with the metaphysics of the Greeks." A transformation of the personal Jesus Christ to the metaphysical Christ Jesus! Jewish ethics— Moses' Rules of Conduct—to the 'new' level of morality, determined behavior for salvation. The road to Christ Jesus—tells us St. Paul—is in our hands, God, has given us free will and a conscience to determine our own fate by the application of that free will tempered/guided by our conscience, to ensure in our struggles between good and evil, that the good always prevails—this moral path, at Judgement Day, will ensure our Salvation—this Faith process, rests upon our Covenant with God, in a form of our Creed!

In short, St. Peter gives us Jesus, whereas, St. Paul, gives us Christ—the Son of God!

It amazes and saddens me to learn that, not only the West but also the East, have not only, not given St. Paul, the credit and recognition that He deserves for creating a Faith—with a theological foundation, on which it still stands, but also that Faith, gives its followers a hope for eternal Life; but for more than 100 years, the two Christian Churches forgot that He even existed; they, were too busy—in their own ways—devising means to justify their own pre-eminence over the other, forgot the real issue/essence of the Faith itself.

The two Apostles of Christ, were competitors/rivals trying to spread the Lord's Message in their own way, but above all, they were Brothers in Christ and true believers in His God—The Father. It is in this Christian Brotherhood that the two churches failed to adhere to that caused the rift between them, and that rift dragged-in the two Apostles, on the opposite sides. It was a fundamental Error in Judgment that the West Christian Church chose to use St. Peter as a tool to justify its pre-eminence status—the Petrene Supremacy Doctrine—to impose its will and dictates to its Sister Church. In view of the above analysis, one, can make an indisputable case for a Paulene Pre-eminence Principle—based on Religious grounds—His creation of a new Christian Faith, rather than on distant precedent and on great wealth and military might. If Paul, was given his due, recognition—long time ago—the world, today will be much different, today, than it is, and probably, for the better.

The Center for Christian Activities would—most likely—be Ephesus—in Asia Minor—Paul's centre of operations, united East and West in the Center. Certainly, Rome, as well as, Constantinople, were wrong and most unsuitable locations for the evolvement and the development of a new—pure, innocent and full-of-hope Faith. Both, in essence and in spirit, were not only influenced but determined, by the forces of the old and the 'new' Roman Imperium; and by the subsequent wrong choices, that each in turn made. I am confident, that, if Ephesus, became the Center of Christian Activity, of worship, there, would not have existed rivalry between the East and the West, since, there would have been no reason for it—the Center, would have united East and West, in faith, socially, economically and politically. The socio-political union would have been strong enough to repulse any Ottoman Turkish invasion. The need for Crusades would not have existed, but as it is the fourth crusade invaded, destroyed and conquered Constantinople—established Latin Empire to replace the Byzantine Empire—did not last long—the Crusades failed completely in their mission to free Jerusalem. This adventure weakened the Byzantine Empire—what was left of it—enabling the Ottoman Turks to overwhelm the Balkan States—piece-meal—one by one, until they reached the Gates of Vienna in 1529. The Western powers, did not come to the aid of the struggling Balkan States, they, were conquered and enslaved by the Turks for over 500 years—erasing all traces of their national identities and arrested their natural aspirations, cultural and economic development through the entire Balkan Region leaving ugly consequences that are, even today, haunting the Balkan people. These, ventures, established a pattern of conquests—Imperialism—based on Economic grounds/interest and the use of force, as the justifiable means toward an End. A principle that eventually led to two disastrous wars—WWI and WWII—destroying most of the Christian World, and for what?—for pre-eminence and pre-dominance, over others!

Dr. Toynbee, recognizes the two Christendoms as, two of the major civilizations that ever existed in the History of the World. The conclusion is too generous and is not supported by historical deeds especially as applied to the West Christendom. With the advent of technology and discoveries of scientific nature—their applications, created different states, emerged, after the collapse of the Roman Empire, leaving Europe without a center of power, that will hold them together—the church failed—new city-states grew in power and pre-dominance; propelling them to new adventures and conquests of Foreign Lands, in the name of Christianity—God's free will gift, was taken as unfettered freedom to amass worldly material possession—God's second gift—the conscience—the restraining force to man's unlimited greed, was totally ignored—in fact, being rich is a mark of success, a standard of progressivity!

This delusionary quest for an attachment to material possessions, coupled with the failure of the church to properly guide the believers to seek spiritual enlightenment created/resulted in deficiency of and in our Faith in God. We, have allowed, the Earthy reality—the needs of the flesh—to precede and overwhelm our spirit reality; this material domination, eclipses our cultural, as well as, our spiritual developments, without, the existence of both, we cannot build the required foundation, on which, we stand firm—with pride and dignity, surrounded by Nature's Beauty, Man's Goodness and Innocence and God's Grace—only then, can we claim that we are civilized. The Greeks and to a lesser extent the Egyptians did it. WHY CAN'T WE?

PART II

The Four Historical Epochs

In order to understand our human existence, it is imperative to go back in time to identify few most determining and impacting global events that shaped and directed the Affairs-of-Man, their state of being and becoming: that is, Epochs, such as, the concept/period of Imperialism – the Idea based on Greed, Glory, Faith and Revenge, justified by the maxim that might is right and energized by Religious zeal/fervor; the rise of Christianity, Islam, etc., and Ideological Idealism(s) in/of political, economic and social Ism's based on reason, a period of Man's deliberate attempt to design the perfect model of how to rule the world – by imitation or imagination – the design of a Utopian system of governance. The other signification epoch of human endeavor ideals with our own creation; who is He? Who created Him? And for what purpose?

Darwin tells us that we evolved (origin of species 1859); while the religions tell us that we are created by Divine power – Power that created the Universe; hence, science vs. faith! Faith, of course, deals with man's nature and his spirit as well, this, however, constitutes an intriguing duality view of man, a view that we seem to be unable to resolve an irresolvable dilemma a mystery that challenges us to find the true relationship between his body and his spirit; the body we know, but the spirit, we do not – where is it? Two possibilities: first; there, exists the Holy Universal Spirit and we are part of it, it is all around us, all the time, we can feel it but it is invisible, and we cannot touch it. Second, that it is, in fact, our inner force, which determines our will and conscience, that are in effect our true representation of what we perceive, as reality, of what man's spirit in fact is! But, what the truth is, we are still in doubt!

History teaches/indicates (us) that those events which had the greatest impact on the determination of the historical Epochs, their source/base of power can be summarized/categories as:

A. The will to power/force,
B. The will of Faith,
C. The will of/to reason and
D. The will of the people.

A. The will to power, probably the oldest form of ruling, based on and reflective of axiom/maxim that 'might is right'.

The Rulers of this model of governance invoke the right to power on number of bases: I am the best, strongest, wisest; just, etc., qualitative claims invoked, to smooth and humanize the veracity/brutality of the naked use of force. History, however, does not support the validity of such claims; for example, Constantine I, the Emperor of the East Roman Empire, tried to use Christians – their Christian values as a humanizing tool to meliorate his absolute rule, by recognizing their faith and right to worship.

Constantine was never a Christian, except at the end of his life. He agreed to receive his last rights at his deathbed. He never deviated nor altered his Imperial Absolute Rule, which was based on the Roman Axium – one Universe, one God therefore; hence – one world – one Emperor; hence, thus the Religious Affairs were all under his Total Control!

The question is, can such men, who have accepted totally, that use of force is justifiable, transform themselves into Christ-like, wise, merciful and good rulers? Certainly, Not. Rulers like that are never satisfied with what they have; they want more, this thirst for more leads to conquests of other foreign lands – the birth of Imperialism; The Masters vs. The Slaves.

Anything based on brutality and greed is inherently evil and is against humanity, and therefore, unacceptable as a model of governance.

In closing this topic, I'll quote Will Durant's "Tertullian's short paragraph regarding the blood of martyrs, those that suffered and died, confirming the Christian belief: "There is no greater drama in human record than the sight of a few Christians, scorned or oppressed by a succession of Emperors, bearing all trials with a fierce tenacity, multiplying quietly, building order while their enemies generated chaos, fighting the sword with the word, brutality with hope, and at last defeating the strongest state that history has known – Caesar and Christ had met in the Arena, and Christ had won".

B. The Will of Faith, this is very similar to model A, the right to rule, but it is based and defended on much superior power – the will of God; the claim to rule is justified and based on the consent/will of God. The intervention and sanctity of the Divine Authority is as old/ancient and is interwoven with Model A. Invocation of God's will to justify one's claim to legitimacy to rule is of course, a religious sphere/domain of influence and control, which gives the selected ruler, not only the secular power to control the world, but, as well, the spiritual sphere, as its head Pontiff; therefore, the anointed has a 'direct' connection with and Authority from God, that nobody on this earth can question and challenge. This than is a relationship, that is transcendental with the Divine Power!

Disobedience to such Absolute Rulers is punishable by most severely-torture and/or death; but this is not all, the threat of such punishment is projected into the spiritual world, where you are destined to go to the Eternal Hell!

This rule/governance is based on the claim of Universal Absolutism; it is the most destructive and dehumanizing form of Authority, that was ever conceived by mortal being(s); their arrogance and impertinence to claim knowledge of/and God's will is a completely and totally absurd. Invocation of God's will for evil deeds that deny man's right to self-determination is a sacrilege – a Sin! God is not knowable. He cannot be identified, nor defined to us the mortals, he simply is God!

Notwithstanding the above warning, most of the human history has been ruled by Pharaohs, Emperors, Kings/Queens, some Dictators, all who claimed that they ruled by Divine Authority. Two significant issues arise due to this claim: first, this claim of Divine Authority is it transferable to their offspring? Of course, the answer is yes! But by what means/process by blood from one generation to the next, i.e., the creation of Dynastic System of Rule. The problem of this system of governing is the attestation/legitimization of the descendant's true blood lineage since there was no absolute law binding succession to the Throne. Therefore, the Divine will had no Legal Authority − it can be challenged and/or overturned by another stronger force, and it was, numerous of times. For example, The editors of Time-Life Books − Byzantium/Great Ages of Man, tell us, that "of the 88 Emperors who reigned from 324 to 1453 − from Constantine I to Constantine XI-29 died violent deaths and another 13 took refuge, temporarily or for the rest of their lives in monasteries". Some of those forces arose from other faith-based religions, which used the same, Divine will claim to justify their right to Absolute Rule − pre-eminence/pre-dominance claim, that led to religious/conflicts and continuous wars.

In conclusion, I would like to state that we seem to have lost our bearings regarding our most precious values and remind ourselves − unceasingly, that civilization represents our quest for the greatest enduring human adventure of love and nobility and culture represents the encapsulation of the greatest and the most dramatic human experience; and of course, religion, that represents our unceasing quest/search for that ultimate Universal, Eternal place of peace, beauty, serenity and grace.

These, are then, the first two of our beckons, that are based on and reflecting our achievements of our efforts arising from our individual attributes and potentialities; revealing our natural differentiations and the opportunities from their developments, realization, and appreciation. However, this does not constitute a standard of human superiority, but only a condition of their Individual Integrity − a state of social standing, that does not infer/or confer a right to judge others, as to their proper station in the Total Collective Body − a cultural judgment that overarches over our human aspects of our Being − a prime and of dominant significance to us All, the Human Beings!

Therefore, the quest to excel cannot be the grounds and justification for the formation of the so-called Elitistic Social Class. The realization of excellence is a condition and a function of the collective totality, thereby is a subject to the will of the collective needs and desires. Created as Human Beings, we have and claim the right to not only life but also the respect for that life and its sacredness!

C. The Will of Reason. In this Model of Rule, we find that man moves from the shadows of the sword and Gods wrath, to invoke and apply his natural abilities to reason and apply that reason, to devise His own model of governance, based on logic and the cry of the forgotten masses, that hears/feels their struggles and sufferings, a Model that is based on Idealism and Humanism.

Many models/the ISMS, proposed on noble and visionary grounds – scientific determinism, humanistic and utopianisms – came and went ending in the greatest catastrophes the world has ever witnessed WWI, WWII, Vietnam War, the Korean and Iraq and now Syria. This proves that Reason Based Governance of man, is not a sound/reliable base. Reason is not infallible and cannot be trusted.

Reasons for their failures are: First: The Architects of these Models of Rule got enraptured/captivated and enthralled by their Perfect Creation, that they, if implemented, would require impossible transformation(s) in the nature and the essence of the common man; he had to change to fit the requirements of the model, rather, then the inverse, where the model must fit the rhythm and the aspirations of the common man, i.e. The Man, the Human Being!

This failure, the unwillingness of the Architects to recognize and accept Man, as He, is, caused these catastrophes. Second: We as human beings reason, but we have the propensity towards being unreasonable.

Second: The problem here is the struggle for predominance between the individualism – his/her determination to exist and the collectivism – its will to rule, which of the two, holds the apriority position? Is there a functional relationship between the two or are they both relevant in our social collective whole? It is a fact that certain areas of life's responsibilities can be taken care by the individual without the collective overpowering rules imposed by the collective will that stifles/destroys his incentive and will to think, to act, pursuing his right to self-determination, that probably will be lost. On the other hand, the Collective life does necessitate common responsibilities that must be carried out by collective decisions and actions that are needed for all to have since we by ourselves are unable to provide them, then it becomes the duty for the collective whole to provide them.

Third: The problem is the identification of those responsibilities, there is no agreement on this: The left says, the collective umbrella; the right says, the individual freedom! Who is right, as yet reason has failed to resolve this debate and ideological dogma has set in, and it seems in stone. My resolution is presented in Part III Democracy – Its Nature and Dilemma.

D. The Will of the People. We are now coming down the Epoch's Mountain tops, to the valleys, where the people are toiling, living and eventually dying; where the ruling powers should be and must be located – close to the people, in order for the will of the people to be effective in exercising their rights, as free individuals to be part of the selective process, in the selection of those that will Rule them!

We have demonstrated that the previous three Models of Governance failed because they, all, in one way or another, are based on the will to control, that in turn rests on man's egocentric greed – the I, is intoxicated with self-preservation, grandomania, self-centeredness/arrogance and selfishness that leads to excesses in the application/the assertion of his will – that is the use of force, in the form of a Dictatorship!

Usually, these regimes exhibit and are based on and reflective of the claim that they are in possession of the absolute truth; which entitles and places them on top of the social and spiritual pyramid, that in effect confirms their Right to Rule, over the ignorant Masses.

This, preemptive claim to knowing the absolute truth, is ironic, since the humankind is, by our very creation limited in scope as well as reach, to understand the absolutes, much less know them; they are God's Domain.

The question is to what degree, his free will extends until it collides with his destiny – Man's will God's fate!

Enough of these cruelties, it is high time for the common man – everywhere – to embrace and adopt the principle of pragmatism, embracing humanism and both rooted in romanticism. This should be because man was created with Life, Spirit and Reason: those are his attributes that are necessary for his survival – his being, they, in fact, define his nature!

To live and exist in a common social environment, he must possess and use different attributes/competences suitable for that environment; his free will to ensure his proper place in that collective reality, affirming his self-determination.

These natural environments and his needs arising thereof – namely, his natural liberties are different from those arising/necessitated from his social interactions and intercourses, they constitute his social rights. His natural liberties are therefore, inviolate, immutable and equal to/for all men, they guarantee man's right to self-determination – a life of unfettered intrusion to seek and find his purpose in life, that ultimately defines him as his own person – the master of his being; this is what liberty is and stands for, and in this quest, we find his justification to his right to participate in the decision making process of selecting, on equal basis, and empowering those that will Rule over Him – the right of protecting his own existence, i.e., 'The Rights of Men': the will to Live, the will to Be what he wants to be, that is his nature, that is his Destiny!

Therefore, we conclude that there is no conflict between Liberty and Democracy, they are in fact an extension of one another. If there is no Liberty, Democracy as its derivative, makes Liberty as its condition for its existence – No Liberty, No Democracy!

So far, we have established a justifiable case for the common man to participate, on Equal Basis, in the selection process of those that will be empowered to Rule; on the Basis of The Creation of Man!

However, there is a sizeable group of people that question and find this justification as unfair and unjustifiable; they also base their argument on the creation of, as being differentiated in terms of their individual attributes and potentialities, and their opportunities for their development and realization, which will determine their well-being or not in their journey of evolving and becoming as human beings, in a Social Environment. The success or failure of this journey cannot be accepted as a standard of human superiority/inferiority, in respect to others, but, only as a condition of their Individual Integrity; a state of social standing, that does not infer/confer a right to judge others as to their proper station in the Total Collective Social Body – a cultural judgement that overarches over our prime and dominant aspects – the state of being humans!

Therefore, the quest to excel in your differentiated categories/talents cannot be the grounds and the justification for the creation of the so-called Elitism, a Social Class, that presumes entitlement to rule over the Ignorant Masses; a presumption that reveals, its ignorance of knowing the difference between the Creation of Man and His Becoming – We celebrate both but for different reasons!

PART III

Democracy – Its Nature and Dilemma

"The question is how much can the wrongs of a comparatively few bad individuals be blamed on an innocent majority?"

Democracy is a political system that deals with the governance of a country, state, province, etc.; governing deals with the acquisition and the application of power; power is the ability to control behavior by altering the laws of the land and/or by redirecting the wealth of the people.

The ideology of democracy differs vastly from all the other ideologies in that it deals with, and recognizes, the will and the welfare of the people, rather than the will and the interests of the few.

Its foundation is built on the fundamental propositions that:

1. People are mature enough to govern themselves without a master.
2. People are wise enough to know their own interests.
3. People can trust and entrust each other with the power to govern.
4. All people are equal in the governing process and the laws of the land.

Democracy cannot exist until, and could not exist unless people – the common person – did not acquire and build self-confidence and worth to fully comprehend and embrace the above truths. It has taken people centuries of toil, hardship, oppression, degradation, abuse and warfare to reach the realization that intelligence and worthiness are not hereditary traits reserved for the elite, but are acquired traits available to *all* human beings!

By necessity, any political party must embrace and be founded on the principles of moderation, tolerance, pluralism (acceptance of varieties of belief and opinion), inclusiveness (a home for all), humanism (the treatment and acceptance of each individual with respect, dignity and independence), and on customs that are based on our traditional beliefs and ethical values. In short "the aim of a free society must be to create the conditions necessary for the higher moral development of its citizens. The basis for social action, legislation and standard for judgment was the common good. The function of the state, therefore was to create opportunity and freedom for the individual, to maintain those conditions conducive to the moral life and to allow the expression of a system of rights in the interests of all." – T.H. Green (1836-1882).

Political parties, by their very nature are divisive and tend towards extremes; however, especially in Democracy, they are necessary and welcomed. Parties offer the people a choice of political options of how the country will be governed; also their existence helps Democracy redefine itself into a more perfect process of governing ideology. Only democratic states tolerate varying political views and opinions, where people freely elect their government and affect changes in the governing process peacefully, according to the will of the people. Democracy, by embracing the principle of Majority rule, forces extreme parties to move closer to the center, where the majority of the votes are, if they wish to be elected, or entrusted with the power to govern.

Today, most people find the idea of democracy appealing, but have difficulties accepting the fundamental propositions when applied to their neighbors. Because of this, even today, most of the world is governed by non-democratic regimes. In countries where the majority of the people have embraced these fundamental propositions as self-evident, democracy not only exists, but also flourishes.

At the dawn of human existence, human beings instinctively sought each other, banding together in groups, clans and tribes, and later into more organized social entities, such as, families, communities, states and countries, creating a communal life that facilitated their procreation and insured their survival.

The success of such a living depended upon and required of each individual to alter his or her own behavior by agreeing to compromise, or give-up, some of his/her habits, ways, freedoms and beliefs. This, in order to facilitate the new social, common environment where all will harmoniously enjoy the benefits that will accrue thereof, such as love, companionship and friendship; intellectual, social, economic and spiritual opportunities, personal fulfillment as well as protection from harm, hunger, disease. In essence, the individuals engage in a bargain and enter into a contractual agreement binding them together as a group/community, i.e. the signing of a social contract.

The terms of this social contract, or the trade-off between sacrifices and benefits, will determine, first the creation and second the fate of, the new society/community. The new society will exist and prosper if, and only if, the benefits for most of the individuals in the new community outweigh the required sacrifices that each must make for the common existence. It is the individual's choice therefore that creates the social order. If this social order is to function smoothly and efficiently, to make the best contract the individual must be free! Thus freedom is the cornerstone of the democratic society.

Social living is not free; it is very costly, especially when the individual is compelled to accept an agreement where the cost, with respect to the benefits, is too great so that the incentive is no longer there. In such cases, the individual has two options, either 1) stay and suffer or 2) try to change the terms of the contract whether by force or peaceful means.

Under totalitarian systems, the means is force – Revolution! Under democracy, the means is a peaceful - Evolution. Here, the individual is not only free to negotiate the best deal he/she possibly can, i.e. deciding the cost of belonging, but is also part of the side that decides the benefits. The individual is the dominant figure; it is he/she that decides and that decision determines the fate of the community. This is the hidden strength of democracy - the strength of the society depends on, and reflects, the strength of its individuals. Democratic society is a place where individuals band together to do things (together), which they cannot do on their own, for the benefit of all: by giving up some of their productive resources to create social institutions, such as schools, hospitals, courts, roads, etc., as vehicles through which to provide the required collective goods and services that they cannot provide on an individual basis. In democratic societies, social institutions are the vehicles or the means via which its citizens acquire and realize their human potential. It is the individuals that are living entities with their own lives and purpose, or the end. Thus here: the individual is the Means as well as the End!

Under the authoritarian societies, social institutions are perceived as something much more than just a means to an end. The government, which controls all, is perceived as an entity of its own – a living and separate reality. Here, the governing elite erects large and powerful institutions to intimidate, frighten and suppress the rights and freedoms of individuals for the purpose of total control of all. The individual is perceived and treated as a helpless being, not too intelligent, at risk, insecure and certainly not to be trusted with the responsibility of government. His/Her only hope of survival and well being lies within the governing social umbrella: the Party. It is the Party – the political ideology's organ – that sets the social, political and ethical agenda and the rules of behavior, thought and belief, whereby the individual is reshaped and molded into the party's image, i.e. the New Soviet Man under the USSR and the Superman under fascist Germany, etc. The state is the social umbrella where the survival of the umbrella depends on complete submission and the subjugation of all individuals to the will of the ruling party. The individual's responsibility is to live and work to ensure the continuous existence of the state – the living entity. And in the bosom of that entity, the survival and well being of the individual is assured: the State is the End; the Individual is the Means!

In order for us to establish our political philosophical-foundation and its ideological orientation, we must begin with man, i.e. the nature of man and his society: the State. Who better to start with than Jean-Jacques Rousseau (1712-1778)? In his social contract he states the fundamental and basic problem that we face and wish to solve: "The problem is to find a form of association which will defend and protect with the whole common force the person and goods of each associate and in which each, while uniting himself with all, may still obey himself alone, and remain as free as before." And, of course, Rousseau offers a solution to the problem that he posed, as did many others, with different variations and qualifications on the social contract theme. Essentially, what we need to do is to define and establish a formal, working, and precise or "best" relationship between the individual and the society in which he belongs and lives. In fact, we have two identities living together occupying the same space, breathing the same air and sharing the same resources, trying to live in harmony, peace, tranquility and happiness, each insisting on their a priori importance, independence and freedom for their own identity.

Much has been written and more has been proposed as the perfect solution to the above stated problem, ranging from the Absolute Sovereign to Utopia to anarchism, in each case with little success. We are still in search of the perfect state. Perhaps the reason for this is that, as humans we refuse to admit our imperfections and deficiencies. Possibly, we may still be in our evolutionary stage, that of evolving towards perfection, which will take a long time. That is why we should accept ourselves as we are and stop trying to improve on Nature, the Creator. We are what Nature/the Creator meant us to be and that is good enough!

In order to understand our lives together, in a social framework, we need to better understand that which nature has created and that which man has made. Nature made man; man-made society and we all live in that social environment, where all of us were born. This is our reality and it is in this reality that we must create the best life for all. We need to make a distinction between the nature of man and the essence of man in order to reach an agreement on the difference between essential needs versus "other" needs/wants of man, then set priories on needs and assign corresponding responsibilities to individuals or institutions for their fulfillment, all within the limitations of our means. That is, make a distinction between man's natural endowments and his needs arising thereof; namely, his natural freedoms; from those arising from his social interactions and intercourses, his social rights. In short, man has natural freedoms and social rights.

By the grace of God, man was created free, and by the will of God, man was given:

Life -- the will to live and procreate
Spirit -- the breath of life
Reason -- the intelligence by which to ensure his survival.

Thus, man is endowed with free

- ❖ Conscience
- ❖ Thought
- ❖ Faith
- ❖ Will

These then are Man's Natural Freedoms – sacred, inalienable, and immutable - and are equal to, and for, all men; they identify and define man as a human being, i.e. the homosapien.

Man's natural freedoms constitute the foundation of man's essence. Man is what man wills himself to be, what he makes himself; however, this can occur only in a social environment; an arrangement between the individual and the group, creating formal institutions, with power to establish rules, rights, for common living; hence the rules, as applied or misapplied to each individual are his social rights and obligations; they vary and change with time and social circumstance and degree of civilization. It follows, from the above, that all men are entitled to equal freedoms but not necessarily equal rights. Our first priority and responsibility as a society is to ensure that what nature created, man shall not destroy. Thomas Paine (1737-1809) tells us "nature made him (man) for social life, she fitted him for the station she intended. In all cases she made his natural wants greater than his individual powers." And since no individual on his own, is capable of supplying or satisfying all of his wants, he is compelled to form a society. Paine, further states that nature "not only forced man into society by a diversity of wants, which the reciprocal aid of each other can supply, but she has implanted in him a system of social affections, which though not necessary to his existence, are essential to his happiness. There is no period in life when this love for society ceases to act. It begins and ends with our beings."

A great deal has been written on the nature of the exact creation of the state, Paine feels that it is in the nature of man to live in common, therefore he is compelled to do so; but what are the conditions that man agreed to in order to join the other men, poses an intriguing question! Was there a social contract? In fact, today, we all live in a social environment and none of us has signed a social contract. The same thing can be said about the primitive man, but is it true?

In the beginning, as the core family expanded into distant cousins, clans emerged and were later replaced by bigger tribes. To survive, the members of the tribe were independent and free, free to leave the tribe, but chose to stay and did so on their own volition. By so doing, they agreed to abide by the tribe's rules and conditions, a verbal agreement freely entered into, freely carried out. The interdependence of each on the rest made each an important and integral part of the whole, giving each a role and a say in the decision making process; in effect a "vote", not unlike a citizenship right, and the beginning of Democracy; the most simple, the most pure and the most effective social contract; this is our original social contract.

With time, the growth and the development of the tribe, bigger and bigger tribes emerged and finally became city, states, nations and empires. More people, advancement of knowledge, new discoveries, etc., made it possible to create and produce more wealth, wetting the appetite of many for more; not only to procure more, but assure its continuity that led to perpetual and restless desire for power, which lead to civil, and eventually global, wars. This in turn intensified the need for stronger and bigger states. Ruled by power and sovereign authority, creating huge governments with bureaucracy and police force and control, putting an end to propinquity, intimacy, trust, usefulness and need that existed among the tribal members, and in effect, the end to "democracy". From then on, "the dissolute condition of masterless men" required that the masses be ruled by force, and the select few, invoking all sorts of reasons and excuses - the imperative of divine authority, wisdoms, heredity, experience, skills, etc., but power was the basis for rule in all cases. Of course, everything was done in the name of the people, for the good of the people, promising perfect life by the Utopians, the Visionaries, scientific certitudes, historical imperatives, purity of race, Grace of God, nationalism, etc. all in turn failed, but did succeed in enslaving and degrading man, his whole being, creating a society - a state that has sovereign power that is absolute and inviolable, united, has common identity, its own life and has its own will [Rousseau]. Further, Hobbes asserts that the state power was that 'mortal god to which we owe under the immortal God our peace and defense", and "the state has the right to force the individual to obey in order to be free". Rousseau further states "another advantage to the individual of being in the civil state, a moral liberty, which alone makes him truly master of himself; for the mere impulses of appetite is slavery, while obedience to a law which we prescribe to ourselves is liberty". To accomplish this exchange of natural liberty for civil liberty, the individual is required to "put his person and all his power in common under the supreme direction of the general will, and in our corporate capacity, we receive each member as an indivisible part of the whole". To claim a gift of moral liberty by a civil society implies that morality is a social phenomenon, which is entirely erroneous. Man was aware of right and wrong, good and bad, before the existence of the so-called civil society. Besides, morality is primarily a natural phenomenon, the individual's conscience, thought and faith. If civil society insists that morality is its creation, then it has to claim Stalin, Hitler, Saddam, etc. as its most moral, civil members, since they are its rulers.

The attempt by the Great Thinkers to find the ultimate and the enduring solution to men's quest for a perfect society has led many to make erroneous assumptions, suppositions, propositions and conclusions about man's nature, his essence, his beliefs, society and his place in it, and the consequential results thereof have been disappointing, and in many instances disastrous. The state of mankind's condition is neither good nor strong; madmen still rule most of the world. Is that the best civil society can do?

It is great thinkers like Rousseau, Hobbes, etc., intellectuals who give dictators their philosophical propositions and arguments, which they use to justify their own personal ambitious zeal for power, to create great states of power where the individual, instead of being an indivisible part of the whole, becomes instead overwhelmed and over-dominated by it. He becomes an insignificant, useless and dependent servant - a slave of the state. A state, with general will of its own, a living entity headed by an absolute sovereign that is restrained in the use of power only by "as it is, does not and cannot exceed the limits of general conventions" - the King can do no wrong! But he does, and many that did wrong were not even Kings.

Whatever we do, however we twist things, the facts are that by joining together men cannot and will not create a state that has divine attributes; a living, sacred entity that elevates one of its own mortal members to a position of sovereign, sacred and absolute, with divine authority, whose embrace, love and kindness brings happiness and everlasting joy to all. All we have created is a monster dictator and an enslaved people, because for such a state to exist, it must have perfect order, perfect fit and perfect harmony, like the human body where each part performs its function with precision, in harmony with others, enabling the whole to work, and it in turn supports and feeds its parts, like clockwork. To create such a working mechanism, a social body, will require the complete destruction--the enslavement and subjugation of all the individuals' wills and purposes, relegating each to be a human cog in a great big state machine. The world, in fact, has been and still is being run, by such social machines, with the exception of few democracies, which with extraordinary effort, sacrifice and wisdom freed themselves from this social demon. To build something noble and good requires noble deeds and free people; you cannot build it on the suffering, pain, fear and torture of others. Only free people, with free will, passion and dedication can provide and unleash their creative skills and energies to build extraordinary things, for themselves and others. The slave, on the other hand, is not a builder, but a survivor, he is a prisoner with a prisoner's mentality: no morals, but only the "ethics" to live another day (a day for a day). The more people you enslave, the greater the aggregate ethics of survival. No future to worry about because they have no future, and where there is no hope for tomorrow, there is no today! This is the built-in destructive mechanism that all totalitarian systems have and share in common, and it is their inevitable and inescapable destroyer, those that dare oppose and alter nature are in turn destroyed by it!

God created everything, and with a purpose. And God created man with a mission, to safeguard the Divine Spirit that he entrusted into him - this is what makes man's nature unique and whole. No social organization, when formed, is endowed with Divine Spirit and is therefore immutable, has natural freedoms that give it moral authority to insist that the individual surrenders all of his natural freedoms to the collective body, and submerse himself totally in it - the greater whole. This is impossible. Man, a natural whole, cannot be submersed, nor conjoined with an entity that is not in the same kind or degree, merely a man created social organization, created for man's convenience to enable him to improve his worldly lot, thereby improving his chances of survival and the propagation of his species.

In this, however, lies man's inner conflict. By nature he is whole and free, but by instinct he needs others to exist, to procreate, thus living in a dilemma--a struggle between his will for freedom and his need for others! The resolution to this dilemma lends itself to varieties of different ideological, political solutions: nationalism, for example, finds the solution in the idealism - a perfect marriage between strong willed individuals and a strong willed (organic) state. In the case of clashes of wills, the will of the state prevails, since the realization of the individual is possible only within the state; further, the state has not only a will but also a consciousness and moral end and therefore is on a higher plateau than the individual. The world has paid dearly because of this idealism, with two world wars.

Communism found the solution, in a different direction: the salvation of the working class from the oppression/tyranny of the rich. What the social class has to do with the individual versus society, their harmony/disharmony is not clear, but the communist ideology did manage to connect the two by equating the individual; with the proletariat and the rich with the state--the ruling class--the exploiters, hence the conflict and struggle. But the two struggles are not only different in origin, but in kind. The first is an inner dilemma, whereas the second a man-against-man conflict based on economic grounds. That is, who owns and controls the means of production and thereby the decision of what to produce, for whom and how to produce it, i.e. the wealth of the nation.

The origin of this struggle began when man started to use other men for his own purpose - first through force--slavery, then by the use of land - serfdom, and then by the use of capital - labor. The class struggle deals with capital and its exploitation of the worker. In fact, the real resentment between the two classes became intense with the introduction of money. Money facilitated the creation of markets, hence the labor market, where labor could be bought and sold like a commodity for a price (wage). It reduced men to sell themselves in an impersonal market, where abstract forces of supply and demand will judge and evaluate his worth. That is, man--the living person--became separated from his skill and craft. Once, craft and man were one, whereas now they are two. Now the needs of man and his means are split and may not match. Usually, it is an accepted premise that this imbalance is always tipped against the man himself and his needs, because market forces evaluate the worth of his craft unjustly. This system did not only rob him of his true value, but it degraded his individual dignity and human pride.

The transition from a barter system exchange of value for value, as determined directly by men and measured in terms of human effort, to the market system exchange of value for value, but determined by market forces in terms of output and measured in money standard, was not an easy one. Now, which standard is better is open to debate; however, recent history shows that the market system is superior because it facilitates the creation of capital and capital in turn increase the productivity of the workers, altering the balance between <u>needs</u> and <u>means</u> in their favor. That is, leaving them with something extra, a surplus/savings. This surplus gives the worker, for the first time, the option to increase his standard of living, by spending the surplus on extra consumer goods or by investing in the market to increase his future earnings, thereby increasing his future standard of living. By doing this, the worker not only improves his own welfare, but also that of the capitalist and they become, in effect, partners.

From this, we can conclude that contrary to Marx, the capitalist created an opportunity for the worker to escape the cycle of poverty by providing him with the opportunity to increase his productivity and thereby earn a surplus, which he can use to create options for prosperity, thereby escaping poverty. Strange as is may seem, the same forces in fact determine the profits of the capitalist by determining the market price of their products/services and the prices of their resources and labor force, but they do not feel degraded or exploited. On the contrary, they take it as a challenge to overcome and motivation to excel.

Marx's prediction of the Capitalists' demise based on his dialectic method did not materialize because instead of eating one another up, they helped one another, in some unseen and unintended way. Technologies developed by one were used by the other, and so forth. Furthermore, they became one another's best suppliers and customers.

The erroneous misinterpretation of history and deliberate misrepresentation of man's inner conflict, the world was dragged through an incalculable and unprecedented human suffering, misery, pain and sacrifice. And all for what? To satisfy an old man's vanity of his understanding of the history of mankind! So what happened to the working class when the state took possession and control of the means of production? Was he transformed into the new Soviet Man and lived in the communist ideal state? Certainly not. Even today, by Lenin's own admission, we do not know what communism was meant to be, or is yet to be, except for its slogan: From each according to his ability; to each according to his needs. Lenin admits, "by what stages, by what means of what practical measures humanity will proceed to this higher aim [Communism], this we do not and cannot know…"

Reinhold Niebuhr warns us of the perils to democracy that "arise from the fanaticism of moral idealists who are not conscious of the corruption of self-interest in their professed ideals".

This warning notwithstanding (as we are not after the creation of a perfect state for imperfect people), we continue our search for the creation of a society with a government where we are all part of, belong to, and live in peace, fairness and dignity. Society is an association of a variety of people with diverse wants, interests and desires, each applying their diverse skills to the best of their abilities to satisfy these wants, confronting each with a maze of interests, claims, and entitlements pressing hard against natural and human limitations. This pressure results in a continuous social tension that leads to instability, disorder and uncertainty, indeed to disappointments and unfulfilled desires. To prevent such built-in social disasters, we must strive to maintain harmony between the individuals' and the institutions' needs and means, through legal, moral, traditional and social reconciliation mechanisms. At the same time, maintaining a balance between the collective needs of the state and the individuals' needs of each citizen. More specifically, the collective needs are in fact the natural freedoms that we possess, and we are entitled to their protection. Personal needs are in fact civil rights that we wish to ensure, the right of opportunity to pursue and realize.

The object of society then simply is the realization of a better life for all via a balance and harmony. Logically, the method by which we can achieve such a state must be by universal suffrage - inclusion and participation of all in the affairs of the state - i.e. Democracy.

Democracy, because it hears the cry of the Breton Mariner who prays to God as he puts out to sea "protect me, my ship is so little and thy ocean so great", as well the proverb "he who closes his ears to the cry of the poor will himself cry out and not be heard". Also, because it does not tolerate a master state, like when Alexander the Great put to the task a pirate to justify the "stolen" possession of the sea, the pirate responded "what thou meanest by seizing the whole earth, but because I do it with a petty ship, I am called a robber whilst thou does it with a great fleet are styled emperor" - Cicero.

These quotes bring to fore a number of moral, social and personal quandaries. God, of course, did not make the ocean smaller to allay the mariner's fears; the mariner is alone and helpless. Alone, he cannot confront the awesomeness of nature, but together with others he can build a bigger, better and safer ship, in the company of others to face the great ocean. The proverb teaches us to share with others, if not for their sake, then for our own. The character of the pirate, the man: we would have spared ourselves much agony and pain if we had seen him for what he really is and not as we would like him to be, ascribing imaginary and idealizing characteristics that have in fact no basis in reality; "a picture of man as perfectible, as endowed with sufficient wisdom and selflessness to endure power and to use it infallibly for the general good" - a saint. Unfortunately for us, there are not too many saints amongst us; "man was, still is, indeed imperfect, and that corruption of power could unleash great evil in the world". Which is the real man, the Angel or the Devil?

Democracy prefers the first, the harmless and the good individual because it can deal with him. It does not like the second, the Devil, because collectively, it does not like to use force to deal with the likes of him. We all have in us mostly good, but also evil. Society as a whole probably mirrors the individual: a large part good, decent and kind people mixed in with a sizeable fraction of evil, vicious brutes. The first group is driven by the will to live and be free, whereas the second is driven by the will to power and to control. Alexander, the Master of the World, driven by the power of the sword where might is right is the Anathema to Democracy, where right is might. Alexander, the state too powerful and arrogant suffocates the individual, his meager attempts at making a living being held accountable and labeled a thief. But he is noble and imperial. Justice indeed!

This quote more than anything else illustrates the fact that in a relatively short time Democracy has achieved unprecedented and unimagined amount of success. It has brought to hundreds of millions of people prosperity, peace, goodwill and hope to the rest of the world. There were sacrifices made, but the glorious and enduring victories have made it worthwhile. Skeptics should be silenced by the fact that we are no longer the pirates fishing in Alexander's sea, but are free men able to fish in our own seas. Supporters ought to be emboldened in that we know that the idea--rule by the people; the concept of universal suffrage and the premise of trust in the goodness of men; the nobility of his spirit, and the decency of his heart has and will continue to prevail over evil.

The interrelationships, interactions and interconnectedness between the state and its citizens must be based on the principles of mutual coexistence, cooperation, unity and harmony, resting on the discipline of duty, law, custom and responsibility. A society that sustains but does not neglect, nor suffocates the individual, and an individual that is an integral part of the community and yet retains his independence of free thought, expression, belief, inquiry and creativity, opinion and choice: A free society, which by its very nature is built and rests on trade--to part with something of value to get something else of value in return--an agreement of trade. We are by nature a species of merchants, negotiating, signing and implementing agreements, contracts, treaties, understandings and covenants, with the exception of our most important and powerful institution, the government, because it rules, governs and controls. The time has come to reexamine its role, purpose and operation and place it under the discipline and conditions of trade.

That is, the government is there to provide and serve a social function, i.e. to facilitate, coordinate and harmonize our individual pursuits and endeavors with that of the collective body. In short, it is there for a purpose. Then let us define what that purpose is and assign the task to those that will govern as their duty and hold them responsible for its performance and success. It is time for us to see the government not as a ruling, controlling public institution, but as a serving, performing institution, with public servants rather than bureaucrats. In short, the government is there to manage certain tasks assigned and entrusted to it by the public. The governing process in this way is placed on a contractual basis, an agreement between the voters - the citizens and the political party that they choose and entrust with the governance, the elected party; its platform then constitutes the terms and conditions of the said contract.

The terms of the agreement and the governing party's performance must be viewed, examined and evaluated in terms of the High Aims and Benevolent purposes of Democracy and its commitment to its people. Therefore, it shall be the moral and public duty of democratically constituted government to ensure that each and all of its citizens have adequate and continuous opportunity to get involved and acquire sufficient physical, mental, intellectual, spiritual and social assets and competences to ensure that each separately, and all collectively, is prepared to establish him/herself in the society, in the form of a person, family, profession, neighbor, and citizen, by being free to acquire and freely use these assets to ensure for him/herself, for his/her family, community and country their existence, safety and well-being, in an environment of customs and legal rules binding each to others, and all to the state, for their life, health and education.

The Government therefore is responsible for the security, health and education for its people. These services shall be provided to each and all individuals, equally, universally, uniformly and unconditionally to satisfy man's natural freedoms: Security, the government shall employ, train, equip and command with sufficient strength a military force to ensure the Sovereignty of the Nation. As well a police force to ensure safety, security, freedom of association, assembly, movement and expression by enforcing the laws of the land, judiciously and fairly to all; Constitutional laws, democratically enacted by the Legislative Assembly, executed by the Executive Branch and its jurisprudence tested by an independent and neutral Judiciary Branch, ensure fair hearing, speedy trial, unbiased jury and judges, and access to legal council and an opportunity to appeal to the highest court of the land, the Supreme Court. It is the courts that dispense justice to all and it is equally the courts that must protect all from injustice; the individual must be protected from the excesses of the powerful corporations, government, agencies and other institutions. They need to establish and maintain that precarious balance between liberty and authority.

Man's security against hunger is paramount to his survival; the government therefore shall ensure adequate living assistance to anyone that lacks the means to ensure his own survival because due to a loss of employment, health and age related reasons. The individual who, after exhausting his/her unemployment benefits, shall be entitled immediately to the living assistance support for up to one year, on the condition that they shall be actively searching other employment opportunities with proof and the assistance of the government, or shall be sent to retraining to an accredited educational facility, at the discretion of the government program official. At the end of the year or the end of the retraining period, the unemployed individual shall automatically become a government employee, as a last resort. It shall be up to the government to decide how, for what and where, the new employee shall be used. This arrangement shall continue until the government finds work for that employee in the private sector or decides to keep him in the public sector on a permanent basis. The government shall unconditionally support those that cannot provide for themselves due to age, health, illness, and infirmity, as determined by agreements/law. Minors that have parents/guardians do not qualify for this program. The elderly that are between the ages of 60 to 70 shall have the choice of retiring or continuing to work, provided they are in good health and their up-to-date experience does not exceed 35 years. At the age of 70, retirement is mandatory, regardless of whom you are or where you work. Those that select to work between the ages of 60 and 70 shall not be entitled to the above-mentioned benefits. Benefits shall be commensurate on the current standard of living of the country. Recipients of this program, and receiving no other income from additional sources, shall be entitled to free prescription drugs, paid directly by the government.

To pay for these programs and others assigned to it, the government shall (and will have the right to) impose income tax on wages, interest and rent, but not on business, property, land or sales. The taxing levees and their jurisdictional distribution shall be the following: the Federal Government shall levy income taxes only, and shall not tax more than one-third of the individual/family income. There shall be no deductions or exemptions allowed. The other two-thirds of the individual/family income shall be used half for personal and half for family needs (roughly).

The states/provinces shall have the power to levy sales tax, which cannot exceed 15% of the selling price of the product and/or service generated in their own province, to be used for provincial infrastructure purposes, i.e. roads, bridges, hospitals, schools, etc. The towns/cities governments shall have the power to tax property and land tax that are within their borders, based on current value assessed prices, by real estate expert assessors. Assessment and reassessment shall be on a three-year cycle. Such taxes shall be used for local/city purposes, as determined by their governments. These taxes shall not exceed one and a half percent of the assessed market value.

The next major security concern is the struggle against illness, disease and sickness. The health of the country depends on the health of its people. A healthy economy requires healthy workers. Therefore, it shall be the joint responsibility of the federal and the provincial governments to establish, equip, staff, maintain and provide health system/services that will ensure quality medical and health care for all of its citizens on an equal, universal, uniform and continuous basis. To satisfy the above criteria, private health services of any kind are hereto prohibited in the country. Professional, medical and health research shall be undertaken by the medical schools at the major universities in conjunction and cooperation of the major hospitals. Financing for the above services shall be the joint responsibility of <u>business</u>, because they need healthy workers, and <u>government,</u> because workers pay tax, the <u>individual</u>, because it is in his/her best health interest, in equal proportions for the following specific purposes. Provincial governments shall pay for the building, equipment and management of the required hospitals and other facilities; revenues collected from workers and business shall pay for doctors and nurses salaries and maintenance of the hospitals. These revenues shall be collected at the place of work and the money shall be paid into the Provincial Ministry of Health and Disease to be used for the purposes stated above. The workers (paid persons) shall pay a percentage of their salary (e.g. 3%) for the above coverage, matched by the businesses by the same percentage on a per worker basis.

The Provincial Health Council shall be constituted and chaired by the Health Minister, called the Council for Health, Drug and Disease Control, comprised of equal representation of labor, business and health and nursing professionals. Duties will include:

1. Establishment of country-wide, basic health needs and standards for the practice of medicine
2. Establishment of expenditures needed and the setting of required percentage deductions from workers' wages/salaries
3. Advancement of programs, ideas for research and development

4. Determination of salaries for doctors, nurses on the advice and recommendations of the Provincial Medical and Nursing Professional Association that shall be constituted officially to:

   a) Certify professional nurses and doctors
   b) Be responsible for the ethical and professional conduct of its members
   c) Ensure high health standards by recommending programs for research and development
   d) Promote the professional skills and integrity of caregivers
   e) Liaise with the Council of Health, Drugs and Disease Control and the Council of Education and Training

The Association, even though legally constituted and licensed, is independent of government control (except by Law) and will govern and regulate itself by its own professional standards.

The coverage, as stated above, is universal so that all Canadian citizens are covered. Workers that have dependent family members shall have a family option package, and those that are under the government's Living Assistance Support Program will have their full coverage paid for by the Federal Government.

The Ministry of Health and Disease Control shall issue its own health card to each of its residents regardless of age. The card will have no picture identification and will only contain the full name, place and date of birth, address and vital medical information of the bearer, as well as the member's card number. This card is portable to other provinces and countries as long as the cardholder is a resident of that province and pays the required fees.

The employees of this industry via their professional association shall have a legal vehicle for appeal regarding their working environment and compensation. For this and other legal purposes, the Supreme Court shall establish Lower Appeals Courts, Criminal Appeals Courts dealing with criminal matters and justice, Civil Appeals Courts dealing with family and institutions rights and freedoms, and Industrial Relations Appeals Courts dealing with contractual issue between labor, business and consumers.

The last major security concern, which completes the individual's natural freedoms, is security against ignorance. Good education and good health of the people determine the living standards and the cultural conditions of the nation. They are the foundation for the individual's and societies' creative and productive power/force. Moreover, it is through knowledge, skills and wisdom that the common person will penetrate and eventually eliminate the rigid social class structure. The upward mobility rigidity has a reinforcement effect of, and between, the four social sectors: social, business, government and education. It is their pyramid structures that enable them to horizontally connect with one another and reinforce one another, this making it 'virtually' impossible for those of the lower ranks to move upwards. Only education offers the common individual an opportunity to break through the traditional built-in discrimination and eventually have free mobility up or down on each of these pyramids, better yet, have no pyramids!

For these reasons and others, it shall be the duty of the Provincial Governments, in conjunction with the Federal Government, to establish, equip, staff and manage an educational system that will ensure top quality education services throughout the country for and to all of its citizens, on an equal, universal, uniform, continuous and a life-long basis. To ensure the equality and the uniformity criteria, private schools shall be allowed, provided they adhere to all the standards and conditions of the public schools and that their existence does not adversely affect the qualitative aspects of their operations, i.e. with respect to their standards, universality, equality and uniformity in and of their programs and training.

The responsibility for the educational system shall be placed in the Provincial Ministry of Education and Training, headed by the Minister. The Minister shall constitute and chair a Council of Education and Training Affairs comprised of equal representation from the business community, the community at large and the Professional Association of Educators - possible 10 each. Its duties shall be to make policies regarding:

1. The determination and establishment of quality standards in courses, curriculum, teaching, training, research and equipment;

2. To ensure equal and universal accessibility of educational opportunity to all the citizens from kindergarten to graduate levels throughout the lifetime of the individual;

3. To set standards, based on ability, intelligence, performance, dedication and contribution to the objectives of the Educational System and/or the enlightenment of men and civil society, for its faculty and its students' performances, achievements and advancements.

The financing for these educational and cultural services shall be based on the principle of benefit-derived. That is, the country as a whole derives benefits from enlightened and civilized citizens; the business derives benefits from skilled and knowledgeable workers and, of course, the individual himself benefits in terms of a higher standard of living and cultural enrichment. Therefore the three groups shall pay equal share of its costs. More precisely, the Provincial governments shall be responsible for the construction, equipment and its updating and administering all the public schools in the country. The business and the individuals are responsible equally for the remaining two-thirds of the cost, which is to cover the salaries of the administrative staff and the teachers, as well as for maintenance purposes. For this end, the Ministry of Education and Culture shall charge: student tuition fees and shall levy education fees based on a per term, per student basis; businesses on a per worker basis, collected by the Federal Government and allocated directly into the Provinces' Ministries of Education and Training, on a per student basis.

A Provincial Professional Educational Association shall be established by the Provincial Ministry, on a self-rule basis, and for the purposes of:

1. Certifying professional teachers and research scientists, as well as qualified administrators;

2. Bearing responsibility for the ethical and professional conduct of their members;

3. Ensuring high educational standards by recommending research and development programs;

4. Promoting the professionalism of the educators;

5. Liaising with and recommending to the Provincial Council of Education and Training in dealing with remuneration of teachers and administration, as well as on other matters of mutual interest.

The significance and importance of Education and Culture is self-evident and thus indisputable and its interruption or cessation for whatever reason will cause and constitute irreparable damage that the country cannot afford or endure. Therefore, strikes and lockouts shall be illegal. These are the required services for the satisfaction of the Individual's Natural Freedoms. That is, all these freedoms appertaining to man in his right to his existence as a man. These services are not only central, but essential, and because of this, they must be provided on the basis of common need by the government, in partnership with the business and the individual on the basis of agreement and contractual obligations; a social contract.

The remaining concern is the search for man's essence, the fulfillment of his social rights; the right to seek meaning, fulfillment, comfort and happiness by interacting, and in association with, others. Where countless activities are taking place and shape, form and create, and in turn, shape, drive and direct the destinies of men; where most of these activities are based on the principle of contractual agreements, as Burke has said, that society is indeed a contract. Paine tells us that "formal government makes but a small part of civilized life… it is to the great and fundamental principles of society and civilization – to the common usage universally consented to, and mutually and reciprocally maintained – to the unceasing circulation of interest, which passing through its million channels, invigorates the whole mass of civilized man – it is to this thing infinitely more than to anything which even the best instituted government can perform, that the safety and prosperity of the individual and the whole depends." – the Rights of Man.

The role of government here must be one of establishing general rules, a legal framework where the individual, businesses and institutions shall be given the greatest freedom and latitude, to negotiate, agree, sign and implement contractual agreements that affect them and their interests. Such agreements by definition, the nature of their product or service, are not universal and uniform and thereto are outside the domain of Man's

Natural Freedoms. Here the individual is supreme, left to his own devices, applying his skills and energies in pursuit of his own interests, hopes, ambitions and dreams; free to trade in a competitive world, creating his own opportunities and wealth to satisfy his wants, dreams, and hopes – fulfilling his quest for meaning, fulfillment and happiness, realizing his own self-essence. The essential ingredient in this realization is the creation of wealth, and wealth is a function of capital and labor working together as a partnership, but unwilling partners, as there is an 'irresolvable' problem that they cannot overcome. That is the problem of how to divide the wealth that they have jointly created – who deserves what? The division of the spoils has made many partners bitter enemies. This partnership is no exception; it is as old as mankind itself and the problem, instead of going away, has in fact worsened because now there is more to divide and therefore more to argue about. Also, the constant confusion between rights and freedoms, and who is responsible for what and for whom; the role and the responsibilities of the government was, and still is, not clear and clearly defined. The partnership between business and labor was not considered seriously, and add to this the economic fluctuations, uncertainties and insecurities creating doubts and anxieties in the people, adding to the problem of sharing fairly.

It is hoped that the proposals outlined here will help resolve, if not totally, at least most of the problem, since we have ensured as our priority the satisfactory resolution of Man's Natural Freedoms, where his basic need for survival are met, and more. This in itself will serve to reduce people's fears, doubts and anxieties and hopefully confidence and trust can be restored in themselves and in one another. Labor and business cannot exist without one another, theirs is a marriage that has no divorce provision; therefore, in order to live together in harmony, they need to improve their mutual relationship: first, by setting up a platform for dialogue on a national level, and on a regular basis by establishing a National Council for Economic Security and Progress chaired by the Minister of that same Ministry, comprised of equal representation from Labor and Business – 15 each – to discuss, debate and decide on guidelines dealing with the issues of common concern and with respect to national interests. For instance, agreement on minimum wage laws, the excess of the CEO's remuneration, safety standards, job security, unemployment insurance and pensions for employees, as well as employers. A pension plan shall be set-up and managed by the National Council for Economic Security and Progress on the following basis for all employers and employees: the employer shall deduct up to three percent from all of their employees' salaries and they shall add the same amount to, and for, each of their employees. This money shall be paid directly to the council on a monthly basis. The council shall determine the precise percentage amount and shall also estimate the employers' contributions. The council shall be also responsible and accountable for the safety and sound investment of these funds. These funds shall be used only for pension payment to their retired members, i.e. 70 years and over, for life. Retirement between 60 and 70 years shall be on a voluntary basis, provided the individual is in good health and his work service does not exceed 35 years. These retirement conditions and terms shall apply to all employees and employers, regardless of any conditions and/or reasons. The retirement money amounts shall be based on the duration of work and the monetary contribution amount paid into the fund. Those that retire between the ages of 60 and 70 shall not be penalized whatsoever and those that decide to stay and work shall not be entitled to collect pensions.

The Minister of Economic Security and Progress shall appoint the Council's members on the recommendations of labor unions and associations and the business associations, chambers, etc. The members shall be prominent and respected leaders in their sectors, with an image of honesty, integrity and ability. This pension, in addition to the government's Living Assistance Program will hopefully ensure sufficient retirement income to enable them to live a good, comfortable and secure life, for which they have worked long and hard and they certainly deserve! Pension income(s) shall not be subject to tax by anyone. However, the most important duty: the council shall have is to ensure that economic and social interruption is kept to a minimum due to labor strikes and employer lockouts. In a democratic society, everyone has a right to free association, expression and organization – to promote and protect their common interests. Therefore, unions and other types of associations are legitimate, provided that they do not do harm to others in their right to protect their rights and freedoms. This sector, the private enterprise, where most of the wealth/income is created, from which the government collects its revenues to provide the services for our natural freedoms and hence our securities, is extremely important. Therefore, it is to our national collective security that it functions, and does so without serious interruption and/or stoppage. Hence, strikes and lockouts of any kind shall be limited to 4 weeks, provided such activities are not in contravention to the above statement, after which the council shall impose a settlement. The dissatisfied party shall have the right to appeal such an imposition to the Industrial Relations Appeals Court, for a final resolution. The council shall also serve on an advisory capacity to the Minister of Economic and Financial Security and Progress, on issues relating to and dealing with monetary, fiscal and trade policies.

These aspects of our economic activities are carried out best on the basis of the Free Market system, that is private ownership and control of the means of production; free and competitive markets that determine the allocation of these assets and the distribution of their output by determining the worker's wages, the profits for capital, interest for the lenders and rents for the renters. The search for profits/gain is the driving force in this system, and the accumulation of capital is its achievement – money is the measure of their success. The premise and the basis of this system is of course trade, and trade is based on the simple proposition practiced by merchants in antiquity, such as the famous caravan traders, Marco Polo's, etc., that is by pursuing our own interests, or better life, by producing something for others that they need, but cannot produce on their own, in exchange for that which they can, and are willing to exchange for something that I need but cannot produce on my own. If the exchange is free and voluntary, then both sides benefit from it. Therefore, it follows that by pursuing my own interest I am reciprocally promoting their interests. This proposition works best in a free, competitive and fair environment; it does not thrive in a monopolistic or monopsonistic environment; therefore, if one such exists the government shall at least put it under regulation.

As stated before, Democracy is based on trust, however because of man's inherent nature towards the abuse of power, we trust with conditions and built-in mechanisms to protect ourselves from those that may abuse the trust given them; limitations to power, such as elect for limited time, vote of non-confidence, press, question periods in parliaments, etc. and of course the division and separation of powers, horizontally and vertically; creating checks and balances of power, all to ensure open, accessible, and efficient government. For this reason, the governing process is usually divided into three levels of government: federal, provincial and local. The Federal – the most powerful – is, in turn divided in two: the Parliamentary and the Judiciary branches in the Parliamentary systems of governance and into three in the Presidential systems of governance: the Legislative, Executive and Judiciary branches. Today, the Executive (Cabinet) branch, its ministerial structure is mostly ineffective because there are too many Ministries – Ministers each holding a jurisdiction that is too small and disconnected to the rest – each Ministry pursuing its own agenda and importance, operated by bureaucrats, dispensing power, importance and interference. The number of Ministries should be no more than nine; each with a broad perspective and focused objectives relying on professional and expert councils to successfully perform their duties, rather than on the inefficient bureaucracy. The Federal Cabinet Ministries and their Councils shall be the following:

1. The Ministry of Economic and Financial Security and Progress/ The Council for Economic Security and Progress (dealing with labor-business relations, economic monetary, fiscal and trade policies);
2. The Ministry of Health and Disease Control/The Council for Health, Drugs and Disease Control (dealing with the prevention, caring for and curing of ill health);
3. The Ministry of Education and Training (dealing with training, learning and enlightenment and the preservation, promotion of the country's cultural heritage);
4. The Ministry of International Relations/The Council for International Affairs (dealing with peace, goodwill and free trade amongst nations);
5. The Ministry of National Defense/The Council for National Security (dealing with military readiness and border security);

6. The Ministry of Justice and Citizenship/The Council for Justice and Citizenship (dealing with police, law and order);
7. The Ministry of Environmental Protection/The Council for Consumer and Environmental Protection (to ensure safe, clean and healthy environment and safe and satisfied consumers);
8. The Ministry of Finance and Taxation/Council for Financial and Taxing Affairs;
9. The Ministry of Inter-Provincial Relations/Council for Inter-Provincial Affairs (dealing with the resolution of disputes, issues and problems between Provinces and the Federal Governments).

In conclusion, we must go back to Rousseau's question: "the problem is to find a form of association which will defend and protect... the person... and remain as free as before." I have endeavored to establish such an association based on the principles of Man's Nature – his natural freedoms and the realization of his essence in a free, safe and caring society, governed by the rule of law; a government with defined duties and responsibilities to ensure the survival, health, education and the freedoms and their rights, where the balance between liberty and authority is no longer in doubt, where we no longer need to ask the questions: can we live in a society that is out of control, and can we survive in a society that is in total control?

PART IV

Comparative Characteristics and Criterias Between Europe and America

	Europe	America
1.	The Nature of Man: Collectivistic	The Essence of Man: Individualistic
2.	Nationalistic	Individualistic
3.	Traditional – The Old	Futuristic – The New
4.	Identity – Blood Based – Who Are You? My Fathers' Son	Identity – Achievement Based On – What Am I? My Own Man
5.	The Father Counts	The Son Counts
6.	Deterministic/Stability	Evolving/Change
7.	Values: Liberty, Brotherhood, Equality	Values: Life, Liberty and Pursuit of Happiness
8.	Constraining Society	Open Society
9.	Class-Oriented Society	Freedom-Oriented Society
10.	Roots-Based Society	Immigrant-Based Society
11.	Government Rules	Government Serves
12.	Inheritance Defines Social Class	Opportunity to Excel/Merit, Defines Social Position
13.	Discriminating Society	Diverse Society
14.	History Matters	The Future Matters
15.	Land Possession – seen as means to an end	Land – Its conquest viewed as pride, achievement – This defines America!

The fundamental difference between Europe and America is the fact that Europe has a long history and America does not!

From this, we can deduce/extrapolate the fact that Europe is stuck in its history and still cannot resolve its past – who did what to whom, whose fault was it, and so forth.

America does not have/carry this baggage, it is a new Country, with new/ modern, ideas, attitudes, expectations and values; and as such, they are defined differently than the Europeans, their Identity is based on their own achievements – based on and rests upon the condition of Liberty, that frees them to, pursue their dreams and ambitions in a free Social Framework; based on competition to motivate and drive the individual to excel whatever direction he/she chooses to go/pursue.

This pursuit for excellence is facilitated by the unique American Social Framework that connects the Capitalism with Democracy – illustrated in Chart I titled, "The Fundamental Political and Economic Relationships of Life, under Democracy and Capitalism".

The Americans are proud of their country that they themselves build; that is why they are Patriotic people; they value/respect the Citizenship of being an American; whereas the Europeans value their past that gave them their National Identity, wealth and social class, based on blood and ancestry.

Acquiring Citizenship carries no stigma/prejudice nor past recognition; it is equal to all – that is why all are proud of it!

The Americans are proud of their Constitution rightly, so, but it is because their Founding Fathers proclaimed to the world that they will not accept, tolerate nor live under Tyranny imposed on them by their Colonial Masters. The Declaration stated July 2, 1776: "when in the course of human events it becomes necessary for one people to dissolve the political bands which have connected them with another to assume among the powers of the earth, the separate and equal station to which the Laws of Nature and Nature's God entitles them a decent respect to the opinions of mankind…."

After enumerating their grievances, abuses, and causes, they clearly and in no uncertain terms, state the purpose objectives, and believes that the New Nation will be guided by: stand-for and believe-in.

It states: "We hold these truths to be self-evident, that all men are created equal, that they are endowed by their Creator with certain unalienable Rights, that among these are Life, Liberty and the Pursuit of Happiness. That, to secure these rights, Governments are instituted among Men, deriving their just powers from the Consent of the Governed…"

The last part of the above paragraph uniquely connects the rule by the People – Democracy to Liberty: it is a defining proposition/statement that man is born free and that claim is unassailable because it rests upon and is derived from the unmovable condition – that the state of Liberty is a condition for man's freedoms which guarantees his right to self-determination!

This proposition, in fact, an Axiom, is the closest that is ever being pronounced to the 'Ideal' Hellenic quest for freedom, and democracy; that leans towards the rights of man to seek the Truth through free Assembly and Free Speech, and through these methods we can derive to the true nature and essence of Democracy as being the true derivative of Liberty!

The American tendency, however, is towards the discovery and implementation of a perfect state of governance, based on the will of the people.

It soon became clear that proclamation of independence is one thing and drafting a constitution that will guaranty the creation of that perfect state of governance, is another; in short, the realities of the two objectives are vastly different; one requires the mobilization and the will to fight; to get rid of an oppressive and brutal Regime; whereas, the other needs to create a New Nation, that requires, the Rule of Law based on fairness, respect for human dignity, and equal application to all individuals of the Laws of the Land; as well as the motivation to unleash and coordinate the human spirit and effort to the creation of a New Venture – The Creation of a new free Nation, The United States of America!

Some of the important reasons why there exists a significant divergence between the Declaration of Independence and the Constitution, in their own words by the Founding Fathers:

George Washington states:

> "Experience teaches us that it is much easier to prevent an enemy from posting themselves than it is to dislodge them after they have got possession." Sound advice.

On, politics regarding the role of political parties, he states:

> "However (political parties) may now and then answer popular ends, they are likely in the course of time and things to become potent engines, by which cunning, ambitious, and unprincipled men will be enabled to subvert the power of the people." Very perceptive, most appropriate for today!

John Adams has a similar concern. He states:

> "There is danger from all men. The only maxim of a free government ought to be to trust no man living with power to endanger the public liberty." This danger, unfortunately, is still prevalent in the world.

James Madison echoes the above concerns. He states:

> "Liberty may be endangered by the abuse of liberty, but also by the abuse of power." Today the abuse of liberty is too much prevalent; it in fact, has reached a critical point!

Alexander Hamilton is concerned that passion rather than reason might prevail. He states:

> "Man are rather reasoning than reasonable animals, for the most part, governed by the impulse of passion." He, therefore, question the need for government. His answer:

> "Why has government been instituted at all? Because the
> passion of man will not conform to the dictates of reason
> and justice without constraint."

The last quote is, of course, Hamilton's that reveals the essential difference between America and Europe, why European countries are nationalistic, and America is patriotic. He states the following:

> "There is a certain enthusiasm in liberty, that makes human
> nature rise above itself, in acts of bravery and heroism."

It is the state of liberty as a condition of human beings that once understood and accepted/ compelled man to rise above himself and accepts the humanity on equal basis, frees him from the constraints and limitations of nationalisms; based on the false premise – that I am better than you!

Because of the above concerns – due to human frailty(ies) – the Constitutional Convention in 1787 was forced to thread carefully the matter of trusting man with great power(s) of control – the British way; therefore, reduce the power(s) by separation and division, horizontally and vertically as well as implementation of a federal system of government – Republican based-rule by the people-state based, i.e., the principles of decentralization and separation of power; as well, protection from the abuses/misuses(s) of power by the process of impeachment.

America, as a relatively new country in search of its Identity is futuristic in nature, it is in motion to be what it will seek to be, which requires change – moving fast, which in turn outpace people's natural speed of change, disbalance/disharmony is created between the two – the now and tomorrow. Their historical imperative is too short to pull back the rate of change, as is the case in Europe. If the historical imperative is absent, then the creation of the Third Branch of Government – the Judiciary Branch will do, the job, in fact, the Supreme Court of United States: 9 Justices appointed – not elected – for life, charged with the responsibility to protect the Constitution of the USA and the people's rights and freedom; imposes jurisprudence all over the country. Their ruling is non-reviewable, and hence, in its totality, their decisions are not as speedy as those found in the political arena; in this sense, it is able to slow down the rate of the speed that they are on, as their futuristic social/industrial objectives requires, thus the rates of change, that cause the gap between today and tomorrow is decreased/offset, resulting in permanence/stability and harmonious continuity. This, perhaps, is the greatest wisdom, that the Founding Fathers contributed to the New Nation!

Chart 1

The Fundamental Relationship
Between Democracy and Capitalism

Democracy
(Rests on two founding principles)

THE CONDITIONS OF LIBERTY | THE DISPERSION OF POWER

(Deriving our) INDIVIDUAL FREEDOMS | (Deriving our) SOCIAL RIGHTS

(Results in)

JUSTICE
(Which depends upon)

SOCIAL COVENANT | SOCIAL INSTITUTIONS

(Establishes our basic and fundamental relationship in social framework) | (Helps us implement these relationships in a formal setting)

THE GOVERNING PROCESS
(Determined by the will of the people gathering of power, creativity and energy for the realization of common and the individual purposes and objectives.)

THE STRUCTURE OF THE GOVERNMENT
(Based on the decentralization and the separation of powers principles.) | THE SELECTION METHOD
(Based on equal universal suffrage principle.)

THE FEDERAL SYSTEM
A. The 3 levels of *Governments*:
I. Local Government (for local purposes)
II. State/Provincial Government (for state/provincial purposes)
III. The Federal Government (for national purposes) | THE DECISION PROCESS
(Based on majority rule basis)

THE SUPREME AUTHORITY
(Rests with the people)

B. The 3 Branches of Government

THE LEGISLATIVE BRANCH
(To legislate the Laws of the Land; establish social framework for peaceful and orderly life in the country for all of its citizens and be responsible for all the Regulatory Agencies.)

THE EXACUTIVE BRANCH
(To enforce the Laws of the Land, equally, fairly and universally for all of its people. The Cabinet controls the Military, the Police force, Taxation, Trade, Transfers, Subsidies, Monetary and Financial Policies, etc...

THE JUDICIARY BRANCH
(Protector of the constitution and peoples' rights and freedoms; imposes jurisprudence over-all; the courts impose law and order and rule on contractual disagreements.)

Capitalism
(Rests upon two fundamental principals)

DISPERSION OF ECONOMIC ACTIVITY | INDIVIDUAL FREEDOM OF CHOICE

THE RIGHT TO PRIVATE OWNERSHIP | FREEDOM OF CONTRACTUAL AGREEMENT

THE PRODUCTION AND DISTRIBUTION OF ECONOMIC WEALTH
(Based on and is a function of the organization and the application of torrents of Individual creative entrepreneurial energy and industrial power)

THE PRODUCTION OF GOODS AND SERVICES
(Depends on the efficient utilization of the means, via the application of power and speed; the specialization process of production; motivated by gain and driven by competition to excel!) | THE DISTRIBUTION OF GOODS AND SERVICES
(In pursuit of satisfying varying and diverse human needs and desires by attempting to maximize their utility with minimum of for sacrifice and pain.)

THE MACRO/AGREGATE LEVEL OF ECONOMIC ACTIVITY

THE FACTORS OF PRODUCTION:	FACTOR EARNINGS		SPENDING SECTOR:
1. Labour	Wages		1. Consumers
2. Land	Rent	Nat'l Income = Nat'l Exp.	2. Investors
3. Capital	Profits		3. Public
4. Financial Resources	Interest		4. Foreign

DISTRIBUTION
(Depends on the population size; ownership of the means and the levels of taxation.)

THE DECISION MAKING PROCESS ON THE INDIVIDUAL/MICRO LEVEL FOR ECONOMIC ACTIVITY

THE LEVEL OF OUTPUT
(Based on the quantity and the quality of the factor input.) | CONSUMPTION LEVELS
(Based on the availability of goods and services and income)

THE THEORY OF THE FIRM
Under different periods and market structures | THEORY OF CONSUMER BEHAVIOR
(Assumes rational behavior)
Result in Demand

Result in
SUPPLY | Results in
DEMAND

OUTPUT AND PRICE DETERMINATION
The Market

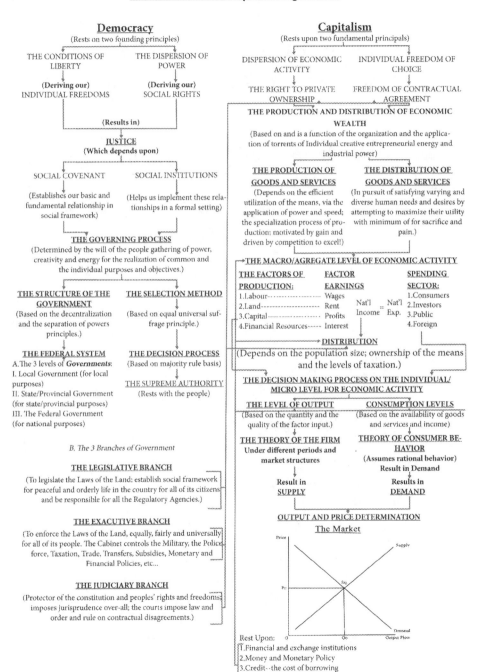

Rest Upon:
1. Financial and exchange institutions
2. Money and Monetary Policy
3. Credit--the cost of borrowing
4. Foreign exchange determination

PART V

Comparative Characteristics Between East and West

	East	West
16.	Culture – nation	Civil nation
17.	Traditionalistic – blood based	Liberalism – Ideologically based
18.	Collectivistic society	Individualistic society
19.	Chauvinistic – faith based	Nationalistic – idealism based
20.	History – fundamentalistic	History – Deterministic
21.	Mystical – fatalistic	Pragmatic – rationalistic
22.	Enclosed – society	Restrictive – society
23.	Authority/security – dominant	Liberty/Freedom – Prevail
24.	One-ness-between state and Religion	Church and State – separate
25.	Identity – roots-based society	Identity – class-based society
26.	Personality driven society	Character – determining society
27.	Government structure – pyramid based	Government structure – flat/ circular based
28.	Government – rules	Government – serves
29.	Land inheritance – viewed as national identity	Land inheritance – seen as means to an end

This chart reveals, if anything, a very significant historical message, which is, that as we move towards modern times, there occurs a fundamental shift of power based on the collective will of predominance in the human affairs, towards the individualistic based preeminence of the human being as the central figure the concern in the affairs of men.

This shift acquires, even greater validity; as we move from the European theatre to the American Social experiment, where we find that the creation of man is celebrated as well as his life in a communal setting, where men freely, united together to create the impossible for the good of all! The individual becomes the architect of his own destiny!

Democracy cannot exist until and unless people – the common person – acquired and build his/her self-confidence and worthiness, which took centuries of toil, hardship, oppression, degradation, abuse and war fares to reach the realization that intelligence and worthiness are not hereditary traits reserved for the elite only, but are acquired traits/competencies available to all human beings!

Also, as we move from East to West, we find that the basis of democracy – the will of the common man – rests on the dispersion of power – economic and political, and individuals' right of choice, constitutes the foundation of the Free Market System, as depicted in the chart: "The Fundamental Political and Economic Relationship of Life under Democracy and Capitalism", a successful formula that promotes incentive(s) and drive to excel through – Quest for/to Innovation; Discovery and Industrialization, which seems to be lacking in the traditional dominated areas.

The above differentiations should not be confused/inferred and accepted as moral/value differentiations, i.e., as moral judgement(s) of inferiority/ superiority conclusions; since these are determined by powerful external forces that we cannot alter such as our nature, geography, history, faith and enduring values.

We, all try our best, within the existing limitations, that we struggle to reduce and thereby create new opportunities, hoping for the best!

The WWII represents a shedding moment in our Modern History, its destructive power was unparalleled and its sacrifices required to destroy an evil were more voluminous and tragic – but it was paid; victory over Nazism/Fascism was accomplished by the 3 Super Powers, namely USA, Great Britain/ The British Empire and the Soviet Union with their respective leaders; Franklin D. Roosevelt, The President of The United

States of America; Lord Winston S. Churchill – The Prime Minister of Great Britain and Tovarish Stalin, Secretary of the Soviet Union – the Big Three, met – held a Conference at Yalta on Feb. 1945, to discuss and determine the fate of Europe/World. The 3 at the beginning unified in Victory and full of expectations.

Roosevelt, in ill health, fighting two wars on the two Oceans, obsessed with the idealism of world order through peace, goodwill, and friendship wants an Atlantic Charter/U.N., motivated by the words of the American Independence Proclamation – self-determination for each nation big or small, and freedom for each individual. This is what he says, according to Chester Wilmot:

> "I cannot believe that we can fight a war against fascist slavery and at the same time not work to free people all over the world from a backward Colonial Policy…the peace cannot include any continued despotism – equality of peoples involves the utmost freedom of competitive trade."

The intent of preserving the unity of the Big Three at Yalta Conference soon turned into The Triangular relationship that evokes suspicion of two against one, but which two versus which one the game is on!

Churchill – the consummate Imperialist: attempts to convince Roosevelt that the two should present a united Anglo-American front to Stalin, arguing that, by such front, they would extract more/better concessions from Stalin, who already has the upper-hand on the battlefield (Eastern Front), much closer to Berlin then we will be. – Conquest of territory being first, matters.

To the surprise, of the British, FDR has his own views and plans of what needs to be Done! Perhaps, because of their own experience against Colonialism – their War of Independence against the British imperialism have acquired and nurtured suspicions, prejudice, and mistrust against Imperialists!

"They, firmly believe that their Independence has brought them such benefits, must likewise transform the lives of people less fortunate than themselves...they have consistently favored the early grant of self-government to all dependent peoples, and particularly, to those still under the dominion of the British Crown; for to the Americans – by virtue of their past – Britain has remained the symbol of all Imperialism...to them Imperial rule contained such inherent evils that even good empires must be bad...(Yalta p.73). Mr. Wilmot, the author of The Struggle for Europe – 1952. Harper & Brothers tell us what FDR told his son, Elliot, "I have tried to make it clear to Winston – and the others – that, while we are their allies and in it to victory by their side, they must never get the idea that we're in it just to help them hang on to the archaic medieval Empire ideas."

FDR not only saw his vision of the world the ending of the Imperialistic Systems but its essential concomitants, spheres of influence and the regional balance of powers as well. His hope and trust are in friendly persuasion and self-determination, where discords and propositions will be resolved in the formal bosom of The United Nations.

In this friendly persuasion, FDR saw himself as "The Good Neighbor of the World." This view of himself, however, misled him to believe that he – with certainty believed, that he can handle Stalin to join him in his Vision of Brotherhood of Nations: this, influenced him to grant almost all of Stalin's demands – Stalin is not an Imperialist, both powers are "free from the stigma of Colonial Empire building by force."

FDR was not alone in thinking about and expecting good things about the Russians hard working people, Republics just like us. Even D. Eisenhower enforced the above view: He believed that there was a special bond between the two countries, but such bond lacked in the Anglo-American Association. That the two peoples had maintained an unbroken friendship since the birth of the USA creation; and that, "There was no cause to regard the future with pessimism.

The above indictment of the British Imperial Rule by Roosevelt is mostly deserved; it is in the nature of the Idea of the Imperialistic Model of

Governance. However, to go to the extent to equate the Soviet Union to/ with United States; and that, there exists a special bond between the two countries; and that Stalin is not an Imperialist; and furthermore that both countries are "free from the stigma of Colonial Empire building by Force", is not only naïve but is a sublime exaggeration of the truth!

<u>One</u>: The existence of the Soviet Gulags and their imposed cruelty(is) is a testimony to Stalin's inherent Evil Deeds.

<u>Two</u>: Communism, has always seen/considered America – the Capitalists; as their greatest Enemy.

<u>Three</u>: Even, during the Yalta's Conference proceedings, he demonstrated His disdain for the rights of the small nations; he, states, that he will "never agree to having any action taken of any of the Great Powers submitted to the judgment of the small powers."

<u>Four</u>: Roosevelt should not have insisted that the United States is free of the stigma of Colonial Empire Building by Force; does He forget – conveniently perhaps – that American 'Colonial' Expansion, based on Greed and justified by the concept/idea – The Manifest Destiny. The Author: of this policy is U.S. Journalist John O'Sullivan; in his Essay in 1845, he wrote the following, regarding the U.S. annexation of Texas.

"It is our Manifest Destiny to overspread and possess the whole of the Continent which <u>Providence</u> has given us."

Of course, U.S. did not annex/conquer and/or purchase All of It – the British stopped them, but got at least half a Continent.

This, American push for Territorial Expansion – the pursuit of their Manifest Destiny – proved eventually to be a great success, but at what cost? The eradication of most of the Aboriginal Indians (the British did that also) and the remaining/surviving Indians were herded in reservations. The loss of a great deal of Mexican Territories and their way-of-Life were the victims of that venture! It is ironic, that what they fought the British – for the proclamation of Independence they abandoned and embraced the British Colonial Imperialism as their model, using their claim to and justification for their own territorial conquests.

The British claim and justification was pronounced in His statement of 1805 by Lord Wellesley – The British Governor of India, declaring in His Forward Policy – declaring: "That it was <u>Providence</u> that "brought the British to India for a higher purpose, to diffuse among their inhabitants, long sunk in darkness, vice and misery, the light and benign influence of Truth."

The pursuit of the Manifest Destiny, based on and reflective of the Ethical Objectivism places the Americans in direct contradiction and conflict, with the ideals of the Proclamation of their Independence, that is based on and reflective of the Morality Imperative. This, then, constitutes the America's Dilemma which, they still can not resolve, and because of that failure, they are unable, as yet, to Define who they really ARE! The curse of the Duality.

In October 1942, Churchill set down the view that, "It would be a measureless disaster if Russian barbarism were to overlay the culture and independence of the ancient states of Europe." The end of the war he also felt that it will leave the Soviet Union with an overwhelming power that will threaten the entire Western Europe, as Hitler did – instead of Hitler, now it would be Stalin!

This was a preemptive move on the part of Churchill, against the American refusal to limit the three-way agreements only to Europe, especially the Governance of Germany and overall European Peace and Security, and to limit Stalin's reach to the Western Europe that he dreaded most, he suggested to Roosevelt, the creation of United Europe with, of course, Britain at the top with Americans at its side on a moment's notice! This, of course, sounded to the Americans as a British design of the New United Europe to be a New European Colony under the banner of the British World Empire; FDR was not in the mood to expand Imperialism but to bury it. This realization on the part of the British delegation promoted Churchill to attempt to drive a wedge between Roosevelt and Stalin by using especially the Balkans/East European countries, as a means —a gift to Marshal Stalin for the Soviet Union's war contributions!

Stalin, of course, accepted, with pleasure, not because that he needed Churchill's approval, since his Armed Forces were in those countries or close by and that his forces will be all-the-way to Berlin, ahead of the Anglo-American Forces, but because it will be easier for Roosevelt to accept this surprise agreement that he considered it as a betrayal by the British. Churchill tried to assuage the Americans' concerns by insisting that the British saw Stalin's superior military position as a fait accompli and tried to save at least only Greece. The Americans did not buy Churchill's feeble explanation and continued to consider the agreement a betrayal of the Atlantic charter/UN, a sinister scheme to further Britain's Imperial ambitions. In the state department, it was denounced as "Churchiavellian."

This, then, more than anything else, marks the end of Imperialism. The second blow came; FDR was so eager to defeat Japan because not only to save American lives but to be in position to prevent the freed former Japanese colonies from being taken back by their former Colonial Powers, – the British, French and Dutch; that was the reason(s) that he was so eager to pacify Stalin, in order to enlist his military support against Japan; Mr. Wilmot states:

"The United States would thus be able to demand that the Colonies which had been liberated from the Japanese should now be liberated from the domination of their original owners…" and this was done.

In his Memoirs, Hull is quite frank about the President's purpose. "We had," he writes, "definite ideas with respect to the future of the British Colonial Empire on which we differ with the British." Churchill advocated that self-government should be achieved within the British Commonwealth." FDR disagreed, he felt that unless dependent Peoples were assisted toward ultimate self-government and were give it…they would provide kernels of conflict." FDR concluded his statement, to his son, that Great Britain signed the Atlantic Charter, I hope they realize the United States government means to make them live up to it."

This declaration, defacto, put the end not only to Colonialism but also, the supremacy of the British as the dominant world power! The end of WWII created the New World Super Powers – the Americans and with Eastern Europe and China in his pocket, a new rising Super Power, in the wings – the USSR – headed by Stalin. The Soviet Union one Capitalist, the other Communist; directly opposed to each other, one based on the free markets and the other one on Dialectic Determinism! Good luck to the world, the race is on!

Which is better? The last one standing!

The Division of Eastern Europe (the Balkans) Between Churchill and Stalin

% to	Romania	Greece	Yugoslavia	Hungary	Bulgaria
Russia	90	10	50	50	75
The others / Great Britain and USA	10	90	50	50	25

This proposal (my chart) was presented by Churchill to Stalin at the Kremlin meeting between the two Leaders on Oct.11, 1944. Source: Triumph and Tragedy by Winston S. Churchill, 1953, pp.226-28, Houghton Mifflin Co., Boston.

Churchill realized what he has done: He states, 'Might it not be thought rather cynical if it seems we had disposed of the issues, so faithful to millions of people in such an off-hand manner? Let us burn the paper'. "No, you keep it," said Stalin. This rather cynical act, indeed sealed the fate of this faithful – over 120 million souls – to live and suffer under the cruelty of Communists' regime for over 50+ years; To the question, what will history say?

His answer – I'll write the history! The Churchill's motive for the gift to Stalin was to drive a wedge between Roosevelt and Stalin by playing on Stalin's the old Russian psyche of vulnerability/obsession with their security; they do not trust anybody; suspect everybody; suspicious of everybody, as Molotov explains it. He states, in November 1940 when Ribbentrop presented Hitler's offer of a Four-Power Alliance for the division of the world. He replied that "paper agreements would not suffice for the Soviet Union; rather she would have to insist on effective guarantees for her security." That is he meant "physical possession of strategic areas related to Russia's defense." And, of course, Churchill gave it to him – in a physical state – the Eastern Europe (Balkans); but Stalin was not to be bribed with so little, in respect to what he thought he deserved – the division of the world in three. He states, the following at Yalta Conference according to Stettinius. "The three Great Powers which had borne the brunt of the war should be the ones to preserve the peace." He further declared that he would "never agree to having any action of any of the Great Powers submitted to the judgment of the small powers."

In effect, it means to divide the world in three: United States, Great Britain, and the Soviet Union. How to divide it, is the question! With Churchill's gift, as an appetizer; he concludes that United States has the predominance of both South and the North Americas, as well as (soon), Japan, Philippines, etc., and President Roosevelt does not want colonies/sphere-of-influence – subservient states.

Great Britain has its colonies and one-third control of West Germany. What do I want – simply, geographical expansion, west of what Churchill gave me, that is, he was interested in securing for the Soviet Union a commanding position in the heart of Europe. Even though, he signed the U.N. charter, the insisted as a right of victory to be given a free hand in what he considered a proper sphere of influence, in particular, Poland – that he viewed as the gateway to the west – the Central Europe, especially the Bohemian mountains, to protect the Soviet Union but more so the newly acquired Soviet subservient satellites. Stalin got what he wanted!

In regards to FDR's cherished plan for U.N. World Organization based on the "recognition of the sovereign rights of all nations", Churchill's comment: "The eagle should permit the small birds to sing and care not wherefore they sang": Adding, that he would "never consent to the fumbling fingers of forty or fifty nations praying into the life's existence of the British Empire". Once it was obvious, that Stalin/Moscow established firm control over its European satellites/colonies, Churchill stated the following ironic statement; he states that "from Stettin in the Baltic to Trieste in the Adriatic, an Iron Curtain has descended across the continent"…(source, The N.Y. Times, March 6, 1946). The Architect – Churchill, Himself!

Stalin's Eastern Territorial Expansion was greatly facilitated by Roosevelt Himself – who believed in and trusted Stalin to be a friend, by being his friend. Both, Churchill and Roosevelt, showed naiveite, miscalculation and under-minded Stalin's cunning opportunistic and devious nature – almost primitive, that the civilized President and Prime Minister, could NOT penetrate, grasp and adequately deal with! He divided them, one against Imperialism (rule by force), the other – due to superiority doctrine for self-determination of all nations and their peoples. Results: America, retained its dominant world power position; Britain lost its colonies and its global dominance/power, Soviet Union won – big, acquired a second dominant global status!

FDR's victory is in the creation of the U.N. charter that is still alive and in business, whereas, the Soviet Union and the British Empires are both Not – not alive nor in business!

A short note on the structure and the validity of the United Nations: I am including my proposal from my book – *Quest for Meaning, Purpose and Eternity – Part IV* pp. (20-125.ISBN:1484188888 U.S.A.

THE GLOBAL SECURITY AND JUSTICE COUNCIL

Today's economic activities certainly cannot be explained by going back to the world that Keynes had to deal with; it is something much more profound and complex, that occurred in the entire eco-political system, as a whole, that caused and explains its phenomenal evolutionary change. The entire value system that determined and defined, what constitutes economic success, experienced a revolutionary change; the rules and guidelines that existed before are now ignored or non-existent. Bigness, now is synonymous with success, but bigness, itself has its own weight, it becomes so big that no one can touch it—"it is too big to fail", a case, of a state within a state—but ironically if it fails, because of greedy incompetence, it gets bailed out, by the collective political will and power, vested in it by the people, at their own expense. The bigness-success relationship induced and motivated two unfortunate events to occur too fast, before their consequences could be understood and predicted.

First. The idea of globalization is based on the proposition that trade benefits both parties—this did not materialize. Certain countries deliberately manipulated the currency exchange rate, to alter the terms of trade in their favor. The rich countries lost the comparative advantage to those manipulators—to the developing countries, by sourcing out to them their manufacturing industries; including the transfer of capital, technologies, management know-how and ensured markets for their goods and services; this all was done in the name of bigness through globalization. All this resulted in the loss of factories/industries, as well as increased consumption of cheap foreign goods; paid by credit, causing unprecedented accumulation of debts—private and public.

The difference with this debt is that a good deal of it is foreign debt—the foreigners now own, in that amount our wealth, we are obligated to them for bailing us out, of our economic difficulties, a characteristics of a poor country that could not feed its people! The reputation of a rich/wealthy nation is now degraded—reputation and trust has also diminished, accordingly. The global economic dynamics has now shifted from Europe and North America to China and India—a tragic situation, indeed.

Second. The unforeseen consequences of the Information Technology Revolution, that succeeded in shrinking the globe into the village, where—I am involved and am part of everyone's business; leads to the temptation of wanting what everybody else has—the imitation factor, that opened the gates of emigration—the flow of humanity in search of a dream—the better life!

Flow of ideas
"   thoughts
"   opinions
"   dreams
"   hopes

Humanity on the move,
Humanity in motion!

These movements weakened the traditional centers of stability and permanency, the political centre of power, gives away to the big global power—the global corporation—roaming free and mostly irresponsibly, in a sea of unchartered and unbridled territory. There is perhaps too much of global economic and demographic action/activity, but too little and ineffective global political will and binding action, to establish a countervailing global force/power, to determine and enforce uniform worldwide rules of conduct and behavior for those unruly global giants of wealth and power. The disconnect between the economic world power and political global will to act, is the most urgent task, that needs to be addressed and resolved, before it is too late! If the current trend of global economic concentration of power continues, we will in time end up with very few world Oligarchs (Russian style), that will not only control the world's economic wealth, but will by that very power, control its political destiny as well. Then, there will be no politics—no democracy, no rights, and no freedoms or justice.

We have to admit to ourselves that current international organizations and agreements are at best, a patch-work of disorganized and disunited points of references; cannot/do not do the necessary job; and the world is too big for a single country to dominate and solve its problems. Given the above dilemmas, what can we do to ensure world order, peace and tranquility? The question is what are our options?

I. Retreat from world involvement—bring back our corporations; impose tariffs on foreign imports, etc.
II. Stay the course, the way things are now, and hope for the best!
III. Assume the leading role in world affairs—rearrange/realign the global alliances, now, before they get too powerful to be influenced.

Obviously, the first option is too late, it is too dangerous, and counter-productive—if we withdraw from Eastern Asia, we will leave them to develop (with our know-how and technology) and probably surpass us!

The second option is equally unattractive, it is too uncertain, unstable, and most likely, we will lose the competition with Eastern Asia.

We are left with the third option, as the most viable course of action; provided we accept the following conditions/realities:

One: Democracy is not for everyone—it is a responsible system of government and requires tradition, tolerance and sacrifices, that many are not ready/willing to commit to—they prefer security.

Two: North America alone cannot solve all the world's problems; it is necessary to reallocate and share this burden of responsibility, with others, based on regional realignment and on the principle of accommodation.

Three: The 'new' realignments will be based on "old concept" of regional spheres of influence and accommodations; based not on ideologies but on economic well-being and humanism.

I. China has already moved in this direction, it has cultivated and enjoys extremely close relations with Pakistan; when the U.S. forces leave Afghanistan, it will revert back to Taliban control, in unity with Pakistan; Iran, is already in that sphere, only question is Syria, if America does not intervene, it will be next; the former Soviet Muslim Republics will join this sphere of mutual interest— they hate the Russians. If the Russians join this sphere, we are going back to the Cold War period, which is not what we want. China may not want to have Russia, because it is a potential rival for predominant leader; also, Russia, as an economic and military power is far behind China and will slide even further.

II. To devise a countervailing sphere, we must include India, Japan, Taiwan, Australia-New Zealand, Indo-China, Indonesia, Philippines—the entire south-east Asia.

III. The third sphere of mutual interests is the entire continent of Africa and all the Middle East countries—preferably Syria included—we do not want the first sphere to access the Mediterranean Sea.

IV. The fourth sphere is European continent including Russian, Ukraine, Georgia, Turkey; the problem will be the inclusion of Russia, since the East Europeans hate them because of their oppression by the Russians.

V. The fifth, of course, is the Americas—north and south.

These five regional spheres are determined on the basis of the size of the population—demography and the natural resources availability.

The mode of their mutual governance shall be the establishment of a governing council (to replace the ineffectual security council of the U.N.), consisting of 15 members—3 members from each sphere; decisions by the council shall be made based on the majority rule; no sphere or spheres shall have veto power; the chairmanship shall be on a rotating yearly basis; Switzerland shall be its place of operations. Their decisions shall be binding on all equally; and shall be irrevocable, and non-appealable!

The Council shall deal with the following world matters and issues:

1. It shall have the sole responsibility to ensure that there exists and will continue to exist a mutual respect and good will amongst the five spheres.

2. Establish the basic principles of respect and dignity for all of the humanity, by enumerating the rights and freedoms of the individual and declaring the limitations and responsibilities of the states.

3. Establish measures to protect the environment.

4. Establish a uniform process for the reduction of all kinds of W.M.D.
5. Establish measures to control the growth of the world's population.
6. Establish rules of assistance in times of crisis.
7. Space exploration shall be a joint venture and the cost/benefits shall be shared equally.
8. Disputes between spheres shall be resolved peacefully.
9. The unprovoked attack by one sphere over another shall be considered as an attack on all; and will require a countermeasure response by the four spheres.

The implementation of these measures—as determined by the World Council, shall be left to the regional governing bodies themselves—This is to emphasize that this proposal is not intended to create a world governing body, and presumes the acceptance of the current national/state realities and their sovereignty rights. The implementations must, of course, be in agreement and harmony with the intent and the terms of the council's decisions.

The selection of the members of the Council—the 15 members shall be the responsibility of the individual spheres—3 members each. However, to ensure some uniformity, preserve diversity and prevent packing, the Council with political ideologs, I recommend the following: Each sphere shall select 100 representatives, based on professional basis, and mindful of population diversity and geographical disparities. Once, the 100 representatives are chosen, they shall gather together, for the purposes of electing the 3 world Council members from their own ranks. All Council members shall possess a 4 year university degree and shall be between the ages of 50 to 70 years of age, while in service.

PART VI

Nationalism Vs. Imperialism

NATIONALISM is based on and shares a common set of:

1. Values − love, faith, compassion, goodness and beauty, freedom, security;
2. History − The historical/ancestral collective struggles and achievements;
3. Geography − physical, country that separates others as foreigners;
4. Beliefs − core beliefs and attitudes, that constitute and forms the foundation of their nation;
5. Language − common, specific and particular way of connections meaningful, amongst each other;
6. Culture − a collective, unique and unifying bonds; characteristically theirs that determines and defines their identity.

In short, a sense of belonging and being part of a distinct and unique group of people that have journeyed together, are together now, and will continue to formulate their aspirations and direct their common destiny together, as ONE!

The essence of the word Nationalism, has, over time, changed, in a very significant way. It begins with tribalism, resting on the foundation of spiritualism − barbarianism, moving-on to deisms − the faiths − different and diverse, in scope and capacity. It is this that formed/established the basis for man's common existence in a common structured social units, which-in-turn necessitates the establishment of boundaries between/ amongst these units; separating them from the others, whereas, in effect, we have created the prototype of today's − a nation/nationalism!

The problem, with Nationalism, is the boundary that binds, that what is inside the social unit: does it shackle, control its members or does it free, value, protect them? The inverse question is, what happens to this unit in respect to the units that are outside its border(s) – their actions and reactions, and their consequences?

We are now entering the 'irresolvable' riddle of the fence; are you fencing yourself in or fencing the outsiders out? Whatever, the correct answer is, the fact is that, once the fence/border is erected, it, in fact, establishes ownership and control of what is inside. But, as population increases, it increases the fence/border outwards – into somebody else's yard/territory – to gain control of additional, useful, resources that will meet the needs for their 'survival': thus, the justification for geographical expansion(s) – hence, the birth of Imperialism!

This historical dilemma – the struggle for survival, wealth and control – the dominance of resources, labor, territory and faith and since, nationalism is the inverse to Imperialism, the aggressor; the enslaver of human beings, denying the right of self-determination – to be free to dream and to hope for a better life; it is then, by definition, an evil entity; and as such, it is in violation of the moral imperative that guarantees – our Morality!

Once you enslave a man, for whatever, reason, you are robbing him not only of his land, but also of his spirit, to be free to dream; to hope for eternal salvation – to escape the confines of his earthly existence and become one with the universal totality, a place of great beauty, grace, peace and enlightenment; this hope then constitutes his greatest motive to become/be civilized human being – that is the morality imperative. A person who is robbed of his spiritual faith, is condemned to the cross of the ethical objectivity, a condition that is a survival determinant, a life that is uncertain, meaningless survival, with no future, no hope, only misery and death – an ephemeral existence!

The irony of enslavement is that the enslaved people in order to survive, they must adapt mutatis mutandis, to the will of their lords, and in time that reality implants in them their dependency factor and, that dependency to submission lasted for over 500 years, time long enough to erase the identities of the Balkan people; and their national identities as well − Fact! Now, liberation finally arrives; the question is to what old past realities are they going back to? It does not exist! It is very much the prisoner's saga, sentenced to 60 years in prison then released, what does he do? Not much that he can do! The world has moved on, new realities to face and hopefully overcome.

The Balkan domination, by the Turks, represents the most profound severity in their brutality and its zeal to eradicate completely, the remnants of their past life's existence; their national, spiritual, cultural and historic identities/realities − for over 5oo years the Balkan 'states' and their people were living in/under the yoke/slavery of the Ottoman's cruel and oppressive rule/domination!

This is in total contradiction to what humanity is all about; it is based on the unquestionable axiom; that no human being is more or is he less than any other human being in the collective environment of existing/being! We must remember that to build something noble and good requires noble deeds and free people; you cannot build it on the suffering, pain, fear and torture of others. Only free people, with free will, passion and dedication can provide and unleash their creative skills and energies to build extraordinary things, for themselves and others. The slave, on the other hand, is not a builder, but a survivor, he is a prisoner with a prisoner's mentality: no morals, but only the "ethics" to live another day (a day for a day). The more people you enslave, the greater the aggregate ethics of survival. No future to worry about because they have no future, and where is no hope for tomorrow, there is no today! This is the built-in destructive mechanism that all totalitarian systems have and share in common, and it is their inevitable and inescapable destroyer, those that dare oppose and alter nature are in turn destroyed by it! This came true but, took too long and at what cost?

God created everything, and with a purpose. And God created man with a mission, to safeguard the Divine Spirit that he entrusted into him − this is what makes man's nature unique and whole. No social organization, when formed, is endowed with Divine Spirit and is therefore immutable, has natural freedoms that give it moral authority to insist that the individual surrenders all of his natural freedoms to the collective body, and submerse himself totally in it – the greater whole. This is impossible. Man, a natural whole, cannot be submersed, nor conjoined with an entity that is not in the same kind, but merely a man created social organization. Created for man's convenience to enable him to improve his worldly lot, thereby, improving his chances of survival and the propagation of his species.

This discredits totally the two propositions that the Imperialists' use, to justify their enslavements of foreign lands and people that: first, there exists a correlation between the territorial size and the size of the quality of the societies well-being – the Quantis Quandis principle; second, related to the above; that once a slave, you have a choice: but to adopt – the Mutatis Mutandis (needs must) principle, the choice, is either be productive or be punished, if you choose the first, it will be good for you and the Empire, however, if you choose the second, the Empire will endure but you may not! That is your choice? When does a slave have a choice? Choice is made under free conditions and on/or voluntary individual basis, both of these conditions are absent under Imperial ruling conditions.

The other factor that contributed to the failure of the two propositions is the imperialists' attitudes and behaviors toward the conquered/enslaved people; their superiority position/condition stood in the way. They, everywhere, believed that their victories are divinely determined – that providence, entrusted these people to them for a purpose, and that was more than sufficient to justify, even the use of force, to rule over the weak inferiors.

Their shameless and unabashed attempts to convince themselves and the rest of the world that Imperialism was an benevolent and beneficial/rewarding Enterprise for the conquered people, not only for their own benefit and control; they further held that, their superiority presence – in-an-unseen way – "will diffuse among them, that were living in darkness, vice and misery, the light and benign influences of Truth", then and only then, they will be redeemed.

Their superiority obsession, in fact, had the obtrusive effect; their attitudes and behaviors, full of epitaphs of degradation, diminishing their self-worthiness and their historical achievements, etc.

Examples of degrading insults and attacks on their values and their faiths: "Good Indian is a dead Indian" – the Americans, – a sign reads – No Indians and dogs – British Club sign reads; "No Bulgarians and dogs – in Bulgarian Black Sea Resort Hotel – Communist period; Ottomans, towards the Balkan people – giaor – Turkish contemptuous, name for the infidels, the Christians; non-Muslims, subject to the Ottoman empire. But, the most cruel and diabolic policy of taxation imposed by the Ottomans on the Balkan population was the "Blood Tax", that is, the first male boy born of a Christian family, is a property of the Ottoman Empire, where he is taken and taken care of, to be raised as a Muslim; trained to be a soldier in the Sultan's elite 'New Troops', known as the Janissaries. They were molded into an elite brotherhood that stood next to the Sultan himself. On the Balkans, they are famous for their courage, prowess and of course for their brutalities, they became the scourge of Europe – Born of Christian faith indoctrinated in Muslims faith, trained to kill Christians, their own families: father, mother, brother and sister and so on! Is this an irony of fate? Or is it a mastery of evil?

In 1865, the announcement of the new British Forward Policy in India, aiming at/for the imposition of British Christian values on the Indian population; this was too much for the vanquished to swallow, the reaction was swift and by the use of force, in 1857, it came, with the Great Mutiny against the British. I'll quote Mr. William Dalrymple (Time, May 21,2007, p.40) to tell us what happened; He states that "Of the139,000 sepoys in the Bengal Army – the largest modern army in Asia – all but 7,796 turned against their Masters."...the Mutiny, "the largest and bloodiest anticolonial revolt facing any European Empire in the entire course of the 19th century". The consequences of the brutal war for independence; "the British destroyed entire cities. Delhi, a bustling and sophisticated city of half a million souls, was left an empty ruin", in response to the Bengal Army's atrocities!

Those that fought in the Great Mutiny, died to protect their religion and their faith, that gave them, not only their spiritual identity but also their identity as human beings! The sepoys lost − the sword could not stand against the machine gun!

India, like Canada, Australia and New Zealand, had to wait to gain their independence until after WWII, as a reward for their contributions to the WWII efforts on the side of the British Empire against the Nazis.

SOURCES

1. The New English Bible—Oxford University Press. NY. Gospel of John: Acts of the Apostles.
2. A Study of History, by Arnold Toynbee—Oxford University Press, London 1972. Parts II-V: VII.
3. The Story of Civilization, III-Caesar and Christ, by Will Durant Simon and Schuster, New York, 1944.
4. A Third Testament, by Malcolm Muggeridge, Little, Brown and Company, Boston, 1976.
5. The Mentor Philosophers: The Ages of: Belief; Adventure; Reason; Enlightenment; Ideology, and Analysis, New York, 1954-56, New American Library.
6. Great Ages of Man—A History of the World's Cultures: Ancient Egypt; Classical Greece; Imperial Rome, The Barbarians and Byzantium, Time-Life Books, New York, 1966.
7. The Columbia Viking Encyclopedia.
8. The Traditions of the Western World, J.H. Hexter, General Editor, Vol. 3. Recent period., esp. section, on the Nature and Destiny of Man, by Reinhold Niebuhr, 1971, Rand McNally & Co.
9. Readings in Western Civilization, ed. By James Dodson, 1972, The Dryden Press Inc., Hinsdale, Illiais.
10. The Epic of Modern Man—Readings by L.S. Stavrianos, Prentice-Hall Inc., Englewood Cliffs, N.J. 1966.
11. The March, by W.S. Kuniczak, Doubleday and Company Inc., Garden City, New York, 1979.
12. The Manor, by Isaac B. Singer, 1979, Avon Books, The Hearst Corporation NY, NY.
13. The Seven Mysteries of Life, by Guy Murchie, Houghton Mifflin Company, Boston, 1978.
14. New Larousse Encyclopedia of Mythology, Prometheus Press, 1968, Toronto.
15. Communist Theory—from Marx to Mao, Monarch Press Inc., N.Y. 1961, Stanford, California.

16. Saint Thomas Aquinas, *On Being and Essence,* Translated with an Introduction and Notes by Armand Maurer C.S.B., M.A., Ph.D., L.M.S. (The Pontifical Institute of Medieval Studies, Toronto Canada, 1949.)

17. Critique of Practical Reason, by Immanuel Kant, The Liberal Arts Press, N.Y. 1956.

18. The Mystery of Being, by Gabriel Marcel, Henry Regnery Co. Chicago, Illinois, 1920.

19. The Essential Descartes, edited by Robert Paul Wolff, A Mentor Book – N.Y 1969.

20. The Social Contract and Discourse on the Origen of Inequality, by Jean-Jaques Rousseau, edited by Lester G. Crocker, Washington Square Press – New York, 1967.

21. The Second Treatise of Government, by John Locke, edited by Thomas P. Peardou, The Bobbs – Merrill Co. Inc., N.Y. 1952.

22. The Confessions, by Jean-Jacques Rousseau, Penguin Books Ltd., Middlesex, England, 1954.

23. The Six Great Humanistic Essays of John Stuart Mill, edited by Albert William Levi, Washington Square Press Inc., N.Y.1963.

24. Plato's The Republic, English Translation by B. Towett, M.A., Vintage Books – A Division of Random House, N.Y. 1961.

25. An Inquiry Into The Nature and Causes of the Wealth of Nations, by Adam Smith, The Modern Library, N.Y. 1937.

26. The Great Practical Theories – Vol. I +II, edited by Michael Curtis, Discus Books – Published by Avon, N.Y. 1961.

27. Democracy in America, by Alexis de Tocqueville – Vol. I + II, Vintage Books, A Division of Random House N.Y. 1974.

28. The Prince, by Niccolo Machiavelli, edited by Lester G. Crocker, Washington Square Press, N.Y. 1974.

29. The New Class – An Analysis of the Communist System, by Milovan Djilas, Frederick A. Praeger, Publishers, N.Y. 1957.

30. Landmarks in Political Economy Vol. I+II – edit by Earl J Hamilton, Albert Rees and Harry G Johnson, University of Chicago Press, 1962.

31. Ten Contemporary Thinkers, edited by Victor E. Amend and Leo. T. Hendrick, The Free Press, N.Y. 1964.

32. The Examined Life, by Warner Fife, Indiana University Press, Bloomington, 1957.

33. The Philosophy by Spinoza, by Harry Austryn Wolfson, pub. Meridian Books, Inc., New York, 1958.

34. The Sense of Beauty, by George Santayana, Dover Publications, N.Y. 1955.

35. Adventures of the Mind – From the Saturday Evenings Post, edited by Richard Thruelsen and John Kobler. Vintage Books – A Division of Random House. N.Y. 1960.

36. The Concept of the Mind, by Gilbert Ryle, Barnes +Noble. New York, N.Y. 1949.

37. The Captive Mind, by Czeslaw Milosz, Vintage Books – A Division of Random House. New York, N.Y. 1951.

38. The Quest for Utopia – An Anthology of Imaginary Societies, by Glenn Negley and J. Max Patrick. Anchor Books. Doubleday + Company Inc. Garden City, N.Y. 1962.

39. Utopia or Oblivion: Prospects for Humanity, by R. Buckminster Fuller. Boston Books, N.Y. 1969.

40. Beyond Freedom and Dignity, by B.F. Skinner, Vintage Books – A Division of Random House, N.Y. 1971.

41. Experience and Education, by John Dewey. Collier Books, N.Y. 1963.

42. The Origin of Species, by Charles Darwin, Washington Square Press, N.Y. 1963.

43. Economic Philosophy, by Joan Robinson. A Doubleday Anchor Books, N.Y. 1964.

44. The Development of Economic Doctrines: The Economy and Its Problems, Vol. II. by Howard L. Balsley. Littlefield, Adams and Co. New Jersey. 1961.

45. Readings in Economic Doctrines, by Alexander Gray, Longmans, Green and co. New York,1933.

46. Capitalism and Freedom, Milton Friedman, The University of Chicago Press, Chicago, Illinois.1962.

47. Capitalism: The Unknown Ideal, Ayn Rand, The New American Library, N.Y. 1962.

48. The Road to Serfdom, F.A. Hayek, Routledge and Kegan Paul Ltd, London. 1943.

49. Alternatives to Serfdom, John Maurice Clark, 2nd Ed. Vintage Books, N.Y. 1960.

50. A Documentary History of the United States, Richard D. Heffner, Mentor Books, N.Y. 1956.

51. The City of God, by Augustine, Edited by David Knowles, Penguin Books, N.Y. 1972.

52. U.S. News and World Report, Mysteries of Faith—The Prophets Special Edition, 2006, Washington, D.C.

53. Time Journal, Time Canada Ltd., Toronto, Canada, 2003. Vol162, No. 25.

54. Time Commemorative Issue—Pope John Paul II—1920-2005, Canadian Edition, April 11, 2005, Toronto.

55. The struggle for Europe by Chester Wilmot, Harper and Brothers.

56. The Yalta Conference—Problems in American Civilization. Readings Amherst College, D.C. Heath and Company, Boston.. Edited by Richard F. Fenno, Jr.1955.

57. The Second World War: Triumph and Tragedy, by Winston S. Churchill. Published by Houghton Mifflin Company 1953. Boston, USA. (p.227).

58. Founding Fathers, Centennial Media, Publishers: Ben Harris and Sebastian, 2017, New York, N.Y. U.S.A.

Printed in the United States
By Bookmasters